KU-612-514

OUT
of the
ARK

AN ANTHOLOGY OF ANIMAL VERSE

OUT of the ARK

compiled by Gwendolyn Reed

drawings by Gabriele Margules

LONGMAN YOUNG BOOKS

LONGMAN GROUP LIMITED
London

Associated companies, branches and representatives throughout the world

First published 1968
First English edition 1970

SBN 582 15283 6

Printed in Great Britain by
Lowe & Brydone (Printers) Ltd., London

ACKNOWLEDGMENTS

I gratefully acknowledge the permission to reprint the following poems:

Conrad Aiken: "Do not believe your Shakespeare's grief", (from "The Argument") "With myriad voices grass was filled", (from "John Deth"), from *Collected Poems* by Conrad Aiken. Copyright 1953 by Conrad Aiken. Reprinted by permission of Oxford University Press, Inc. and Brandt & Brandt.

Alcman: "Vesper", *Anyte*: "The Dolphin's Tomb", from *Greek Poetry for Everyman* by F. L. Lucas. Reprinted by permission of J. M. Dent & Sons Ltd.

Anonymous: "Book-Moth", "The Whale", from *An Anthology of Old English Poetry*, translated by Charles W. Kennedy. Copyright © 1960 by Oxford University Press, Inc. Reprinted by permission. "Erin (Elephant)", from *Poems from Black Africa* edited by Langston Hughes. By permission of Indiana University Press. "The Icebound Swans", from *The Silver Branch* by Sean O'Faolain, Jonathan Cape Ltd. By permission of Sean O'Faolain. "The Monk and his Cat", from *The Irish Tradition* by Robin Flower. By permission of The Clardendon Press, Oxford. "The Unicorn's Hoofs!", from *The Book of Songs* translated by Arthur Waley. By permission of George Allen & Unwin Ltd.

Max Beerbohm: "Brave Rover", from J. G. Riewald: *Max in Verse*, The Stephen Greene Press, Brattleboro, Vt. Copyright © 1963 by J. G. Riewald. By permission of The Stephen Greene Press and The Estate of the late Max Beerbohm.

William Rose Benét: "The Bestiary", "The Fawn in the Snow", reprinted by permission of Harold Ober Associates, Inc. Copyright © 1947 and 1935 by William Rose Benét.

Edmund Blunden: "The Pike", from *Poems of Many Years*, William Collins Sons & Co. Ltd. Reprinted by permission of A. D. Peters & Co.

Robert Bridges: "I heard a linnet courting", "Nightingales", from *Poetical Works of Robert Bridges*, 1936. By permission of The Clarendon Press, Oxford.

Roy Campbell: "Horses on the Camargue", from *Collected Poems* by Roy Campbell. By permission of Curtis Brown Ltd., London. "Out of the Ark's grim hold", (from "The Flaming Terrapin") from *Collected Poems*. By permission of the Executors of the Roy Campbell Estate and Jonathan Cape Ltd.

Hugh Chesterman: "Noah and the Rabbit". By permission of Basil Blackwell & Mott Ltd.

Elizabeth Coatsworth: "Calling in the Cat". Reprinted by permission of Coward-McCann, Inc., from *Compass Rose* by Elizabeth Coatsworth. Copyright 1929 by Coward-McCann, Inc., renewed 1957 by Elizabeth Coatsworth.

Robert P. Tristram Coffin: "Old Blue". Reprinted by permission of The Macmillan Company from *Selected Poems* by Robert P. Tristram Coffin. Copyright 1955 by the Administrators of the Estate of Robert P. Tristram Coffin. "The Gracious and the Gentle Thing", "The satin mice creaking last Summer's grass", from *On the Green Carpet* by Robert P. Tristram Coffin. Copyright © 1951 by The Bobbs Merrill Company, Inc.

Hugh MacDiarmid: "Parley of Beasts". Reprinted by permission of The Macmillan Company from *Collected Poems of Hugh MacDiarmid.* Copyright © Christopher Murray Grieve, 1948, 1962.

John Masefield: "Reynard the Fox", from *Poems* by John Masefield. Copyright 1919 by John Masefield, renewed 1947 by John Masefield. Reprinted by permission of The Macmillan Company and The Society of Authors as the literary representative of the estate of the late Dr. John Masefield O.M.

Marianne Moore: "The Wood-Weasel", from *The Complete Poems of Marianne Moore*. Reprinted by permission of Faber and Faber Ltd.

Christian Morgenstern: "The Mousetrap", "Vice-Versa", from *An Anthology of German Poetry from Hölderlin to Rilke in English Translation,* edited by Angel Flores, Anchor Books. Copyright © by Angel Flores. "She-Goat and Glow-Worm", from *Modern German Poetry 1910-1960.* Copyright © 1962 by Michael Hamburger and Christopher Middleton. By permission of MacGibbon & Kee Ltd.

Kenneth Patchen: "A Trueblue Gentleman", from *Collected Poems*. Copyright © 1957 by New Directions Publishing Corporation. Reprinted by permission of New Directions Publishing Corporation.

Po Chü-i: "The Red Cockatoo", from *170 Chinese Poems,* translated by Arthur Waley. Reprinted by permission of Constable and Company Ltd.

John Crowe Ransom: "Lady Lost", from *Selected Poems,* Eyre & Spottiswoode Ltd. publishers, Alfred A. Knopf, Inc. proprietors. Reprinted by permission.

Rainer Maria Rilke: "The Panther", from *Poems of Rainer Maria Rilke,* translated by Jessie Lemont, New York, 1943. Reprinted by permission of Columbia University Press.

Theodore Roethke: "A Walk in Late Summer", "Snake", "The Meadow Mouse", from *The Collected Poems of Theodore Roethke*. Reprinted by permission of Faber and Faber Ltd.

Carl Sandburg: "Worms". Copyright, 1950, by Carl Sandburg. Reprinted from his volume *Complete Poems* by permission of Harcourt, Brace & World, Inc. "Buffalo Dusk", from *Slabs of the Sunburnt West* by Carl Sandburg. Copyright, 1922, by Harcourt, Brace & World, Inc. Copyright, 1950, by Carl Sandburg. Reprinted by permission of Harcourt, Brace & World, Inc.

Stevie Smith: "The Old Sweet Dove of Wiveton", from *Selected Poems* by Stevie Smith. By permission of Longman Group Ltd.

James Stephens: "The Goat Paths". Reprinted from *Collected Poems* by James Stephens by permission of Mrs. Iris Wise and Macmillan & Co. Ltd.

Wallace Stevens: "The Rabbit as King of the Ghosts", "Song of Fixed Accord", from *The Collected Poems of Wallace Stevens.* Reprinted by permission of Faber and Faber Ltd.

Douglas Stewart: "The Bunyip", from *Dosser in the Springtime*, by Douglas Stewart, 1946. Reprinted by permission of Angus & Robertson Ltd.

Mark Van Doren: "Crow", "Midwife Cat", from *Collected and New Poems: 1924-1963*, by Mark Van Doren. By permission of Mark Van Doren.

ACKNOWLEDGMENTS

Reprinted by permission of the publishers.

Padraic Colum: "Otters", from *Poems* by Padraic Colum, 1932. By permission of the author.

W. H. Davies: "Sheep", "The Example", from *The Complete Poems of* W. H. Davies. By permission of Mrs. H. M. Davies and Jonathan Cape Ltd.

Walter de la Mare: "Nicholas Nye". By permission of The Literary Trustees of Walter de la Mare and The Society of Authors as their representative.

Emily Dickinson: Poem 117 ("She sights a bird, she chuckles") from *Bolts of Melody: New Poems of Emily Dickinson,* edited by Mabel Loomis Todd and Millicent Todd Bingham. Copyright, 1954 by the Trustees of Amherst College. Reprinted by permission of Harper & Row, Publishers.

Robert Farren: "The Pets", from *Selected Poems* by Robert Farren, Sheed & Ward Ltd. By permission of Robert Farren.

Robert Francis: "The Orb Weaver". Copyright © 1946 by Robert Francis. Reprinted from *The Orb Weaver* by Robert Francis, by permission of Wesleyan University Press.

Robert Frost: "A Cow in Apple Time", "Fireflies in the Garden", from *Complete Poems of Robert Frost,* Jonathan Cape Ltd., publishers, Holt, Rinehart and Winston, Inc., proprietors. By permission.

Carmen Bernos de Gasztold: "The Camel", from *The Beasts' Choir* by Carmen Bernos de Gasztold, translated by Rumer Godden. Reprinted by permission of Macmillan & Co. Ltd.

Robert Graves: "Flying Crooked", from *Collected Poems,* 1965. Reprinted by permission of Robert Graves.

Robert Hillyer: "Lunar Moth", "The Termites", from *The Collected Poems of Robert Hillyer.* Copyright 1933 and renewed 1961 by Robert Hillyer. Reprinted by permission of Alfred A. Knopf, Inc.

Ralph Hodgson: "The Bull", from *The Collected Poems of Ralph Hodgson.* Reprinted by permission of Macmillan & Co. Ltd.

Ted Hughes: "Hawk Roosting", from *Lupercal.* Reprinted by permission of Faber and Faber Ltd.

Francis Jammes: "A Prayer to Go to Paradise with the Donkeys", translated by Richard Wilbur, from Richard Wilbur: *Poems 1943-1956.* Reprinted by permission of Faber and Faber Ltd.

Randall Jarrell: "Bats". Reprinted by permission of The Macmillan Company from *The Lost World* by Randall Jarrell. Copyright © The Macmillan Company 1964. "The Mockingbird". Reprinted by permission of The Macmillan Company from *The Lost World.* Copyright © The Macmillan Company 1963. Originally published by *The New Yorker.*

Rudyard Kipling: "The Law of the Jungle", from *The Second Jungle Book.* By permission of Mrs. George Bambridge and Macmillan & Company Ltd.

Philip Larkin: "First Sight", from *The Whitsun Weddings* by Philip Larkin. Reprinted by permission of Faber and Faber Ltd.

D. H. Lawrence: "Kangaroo", "The Mosquito Knows", from *The Complete Poems of D. H. Lawrence,* edited by Vivian de Sola Pinto and F. Warren Roberts, published by William Heinemann Ltd. By permission of the Estate of the late Mrs. Frieda Lawrence and Laurence Pollinger Ltd.

ACKNOWLEDGMENTS

William Carlos Williams: "The Horse", from *The Collected Later Poems of William Carlos Williams*. By permission of MacGibbon & Kee Ltd.

Elinor Wylie: "The Eagle and the Mole", "The Tortoise in Eternity". Copyright 1921 by Alfred A. Knopf, Inc., renewed 1949 by William Rose Benét. Reprinted from *Collected Poems of Elinor Wylie* by permission of the publisher.

W. B. Yeats: "Another Song of a Fool", "Two Songs of a Fool", from *Collected Poems of W. B. Yeats*. By permission of Mr. M. B. Yeats and Macmillan & Co. Ltd.

Andrew Young: "At Amberley Wild Brooks", "The Dead Crab", "The Farmer's Gun", from *Collected Poems of Andrew Young*. By permission of Rupert Hart-Davis Ltd.

for
M. J. O'M

CONTENTS

OUT
of the
ARK

A WALK IN LATE SUMMER

A gull rides on the ripples of a dream,
White upon white, slow-settling on a stone;
Across my lawn the soft-backed creatures come;
In the weak light they wander, each alone.
Bring me the meek, for I would know their ways;
I am a connoisseur of midnight eyes.
The small! The small! I hear them singing clear
On the long banks, in the soft summer air.

Theodore Roethke

from *A Walk in Late Summer*

THE OLD SWEET DOVE OF WIVETON

'Twas the voice of the sweet dove
I heard him move
I heard him cry
Love, love.

High in the chestnut tree
Is the nest of the old dove
And there he sits solitary
Crying, Love, love.

The gray of this heavy day
Makes the green of the trees' leaves and the grass brighter
And the flowers of the chestnut tree whiter
And whiter the flowers of the high cow-parsley.

So still is the air
So heavy the sky
You can hear the splash
Of the water falling from the green grass
As Red and Honey push by,
The old dogs,
Gone away, gone hunting by the marsh bogs.

Happy the retriever dogs in their pursuit
Happy in bog-mud the busy foot.

Now all is silent, it is silent again
In the sombre day and the beginning soft rain
It is a silence made more actual
By the moan from the high tree that is occasional,

Where in his nest above
Still sits the old dove,
Murmuring solitary
Crying for pain,
Crying most melancholy
Again and again.

Stevie Smith

THE PETS

Colm had a cat,
and a wren,
and a fly.

The cat was a pet,
and the wren,
and the fly.

And it happened that the wren
ate the fly;
and it happened that the cat
ate the wren.

Then the cat died.

So Saint Colm lacked a cat
and a wren,
and a fly.

But Saint Colm loved the cat,
and the wren,
and the fly,

so he prayed to get them back,
cat and wren;
and he prayed to get them back,
wren and fly.

And the cat became alive
and delivered up the wren;
and the wren became alive
and delivered up the fly;
and they all lived with Colm
till the day came to die.

First the cat died.
Then the wren died.
Then the fly.

Robert Farren

SHE-GOAT AND GLOW-WORM

The glow-worm sings her bed-time prayers.
The woodland she-goat, marvelling, stares.

The she-goat wags her beard, as though
she knew all that there is to know.

She finds the glow-worm's song unclear,
but very sweet upon the ear.

The glow-worm soon takes her repose.
The goat through woodland thoughtful goes.

Christian Morgenstern

TRANSLATED FROM THE GERMAN BY
Christopher Middleton

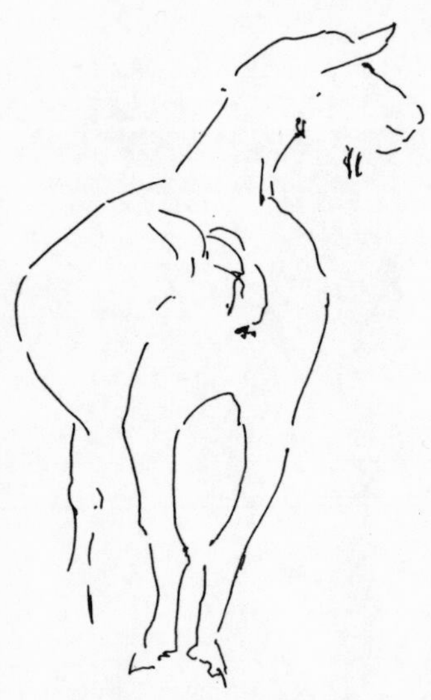

LUNAR MOTH

From the forest of night
Cometh the light
Green-wingëd flight—
Titania come
To a mortal's home
From the low-moon land
With her wings and her wand
And her bright black eyes
And her tiny feet
And her wings pale green
Like wind through wheat.
Now I am wise,
For now I have seen
Men told no lies
Of a fairy queen.
She was here on the wall,
And now she has gone,
Quiet, small,
To the night, alone.
With a wave of her wand
She vanished, beyond
The sky to the cool
Moon of July.

Robert Hillyer

Titania: queen of the fairies

BATS

A bat is born
Naked and blind and pale.
His mother makes a pocket of her tail
And catches him. He clings to her long fur
By his thumbs and toes and teeth.
And then the mother dances through the night
Doubling and looping, soaring, somersaulting–
Her baby hangs on underneath.
All night, in happiness, she hunts and flies.
Her high sharp cries
Like shining needlepoints of sound
Go out into the night and, echoing back,
Tell her what they have touched.
She hears how far it is, how big it is,
Which way it's going:
She lives by hearing.
The mother eats the moths and gnats she catches
In full flight; in full flight
The mother drinks the water of the pond
She skims across. Her baby hangs on tight.
Her baby drinks the milk she makes him
In moonlight or starlight, in mid-air.
Their single shadow, printed on the moon
Or fluttering across the stars,
Whirls on all night; at daybreak
The tired mother flaps home to her rafter.
The others all are there.

They hang themselves up by their toes,
They wrap themselves in their brown wings.
Bunched upside-down, they sleep in air.
Their sharp ears, their sharp teeth, their quick sharp faces
Are dull and slow and mild.
All the bright day, as the mother sleeps,
She folds her wings about her sleeping child.

Randall Jarrell

NOAH AND THE RABBIT

"No land," said Noah,
"There-is-not-any-land.
Oh, Rabbit, Rabbit, can't you understand?"

But Rabbit shook his head:
"Say it again," he said,
"And slowly, please.
No good brown earth for burrows,
And no trees;
No wastes where vetch and rabbit-parsley grows,
No brakes, no bushes and no turnip rows,
No holt, no upland, meadowland or weald,
No tangled hedgerow and no playtime field?"

"No land at all—just water," Noah replied,
And Rabbit sighed.
"For always, Noah?" he whispered, "will there be
Nothing henceforth for ever but the sea?
Or will there come a day
When the green earth will call me back to play?"

Noah bowed his head:
"Some day . . . some day," he said.

Hugh Chesterman

brakes: thickets
holt: woods, or a lair
weald: upland plain

A DREAM

Once a dream did weave a shade
O'er my Angel-guarded bed,
That an emmet lost its way
Where on grass methought I lay.

Troubled, 'wilder'd, and forlorn,
Dark, benighted, travel-worn,
Over many a tangled spray,
All heart-broke I heard her say:

"O my children! do they cry?
Do they hear their father sigh?
Now they look abroad to see:
Now return and weep for me."

Pitying, I dropp'd a tear;
But I saw a glow-worm near,
Who replied: "What wailing wight
Calls the watchman of the night?

"I am set to light the ground,
While the beetle goes his round
Follow now the beetle's hum;
Little wanderer, hie thee home."

William Blake

emmet: ant
wight: creature

TWO SONGS OF A FOOL

I

A speckled cat and a tame hare
Eat at my hearthstone
And sleep there;
And both look up to me alone
For learning and defence
As I look up to Providence.

I start out of my sleep to think
Some day I may forget
Their food and drink;
Or, the house door left unshut,
The hare may run till it's found
The horn's sweet note and the tooth of the hound.

I bear a burden that might well try
Men that do all by rule,
And what can I
That am a wandering-witted fool
But pray to God that He ease
My great responsibilities?

II

I slept on my three-legged stool by the fire,
The speckled cat slept on my knee;
We never thought to enquire
Where the brown hare might be,
And whether the door were shut.
Who knows how she drank the wind
Stretched up on two legs from the mat,
Before she had settled her mind
To drum with her heel and to leap?
Had I but awakened from sleep
And called her name, she had heard,
It may be, and had not stirred,
That now, it may be, has found
The horn's sweet note and the tooth of the hound.

W. B. Yeats

CALLING IN THE CAT

Now from the dark, a deeper dark,
the cat slides,
furtive and aware,
his eyes still shine with meteor spark,
the cold dew weights his hair.
Suspicious,
hesitant, he comes
stepping morosely from the night,
held but repelled,
repelled but held,
by lamp and firelight.

Now call your blandest,
offer up
the sacrifice of meat,
and snare the wandering soul with greeds,
give him to drink and eat,
and he shall walk fastidiously
into the trap of old
on feet that still smell delicately
of withered ferns and mould.

Elizabeth Coatsworth

TAKE ANY BIRD

Take any bird, and put it in a cage,
And do all thine intent and thy couràge
To foster it tenderly with meat and drink
Of all the dainties that thou canst bethink,
And keep it all so cleanly as thou may,
Although his cage of gold be never so gay,
Yet hath this bird, by twenty thousand fold
Liefer in a forest, that is rude and cold
Go eatë wormës and such wretchedness.
For ever this bird will do his business
To escape out of his cagë, if he may.
His liberty this bird desireth aye.

Let take a cat, and foster him well with milk
And tender flesh, and make his couch of silk,
And let him see a mouse go by the wall,
Anon he waveth milk and flesh and all,
And every dainty that is in that house,
Such appetite hath he to eat a mouse.

Geoffrey Chaucer

from *The Manciple's Tale*

courage: desire
liefer: rather

FLYING CROOKED

The butterfly, a cabbage-white,
(His honest idiocy of flight)
Will never now, it is too late,
Master the art of flying straight,
Yet has—who knows so well as I?—
A just sense of how not to fly:
He lurches here and here by guess
And God and hope and hopelessness.
Even the aerobatic swift
Has not his flying-crooked gift.

Robert Graves

THE HORSE

The horse moves
independently
without reference
to his load.

He has eyes
like a woman and
turns them
about, throws

back his ears
and is generally
conscious of
the world. Yet

he pulls when
he must and
pulls well, blowing
fog from

his nostrils
like fumes from
the twin
exhausts of a car.

William Carlos Williams

A PRAYER TO GO TO PARADISE WITH THE DONKEYS

to Maire and Jack

When I must come to you, O my God, I pray
It be some dusty-roaded holiday,
And even as in my travels here below,
I beg to choose by what road I shall go
To Paradise, where the clear stars shine by day.
I'll take my walking-stick and go my way,
And to my friends the donkeys I shall say,
"I am Francis Jammes, and I'm going to Paradise,
For there is no hell in the land of the loving God."
And I'll say to them: "Come, sweet friends of the blue skies,
Poor creatures who with a flap of the ears or a nod
Of the head shake off the buffets, the bees, the flies . . ."

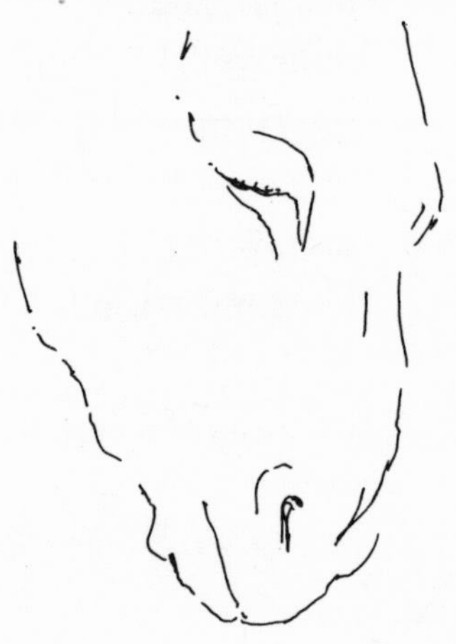

Let me come with these donkeys, Lord, into your land,
These beasts who bow their heads so gently, and stand
With their small feet joined together in a fashion
Utterly gentle, asking your compassion.
I shall arrive, followed by their thousands of ears,
Followed by those with baskets at their flanks,
By those who lug the carts of mountebanks
Or loads of feather-dusters and kitchen-wares,
By those with humps of battered water-cans,
By bottle-shaped she-asses who halt and stumble,
By those tricked out in little pantaloons
To cover their wet, blue galls where flies assemble
In whirling swarms, making a drunken hum.
Dear God, let it be with these donkeys that I come,
And let it be that angels lead us in peace
To leafy streams where cherries tremble in air,
Sleek as the laughing flesh of girls; and there
In that haven of souls let it be that, leaning above
Your divine waters, I shall resemble these donkeys,
Whose humble and sweet poverty will appear
Clear in the clearness of your eternal love.

Francis Jammes

TRANSLATED FROM THE FRENCH BY
Richard Wilbur

mountebanks: travelling quacks
galls: sores

PARLEY OF BEASTS

Auld Noah was at hame wi' them a',
The lion and the lamb,
Pair by pair they entered the Ark
And he took them as they cam'.

If twa o' ilka beist there is
Into this room sud come,
Wad I cud welcome them like him,
And no' staun' gowpin' dumb!

Be chief wi' them and they wi' me
And a' wi' ane anither,
As Noah and his couples were
There in the Ark thegither.

It's fain I'd mell wi' tiger and tit,
Wi' elephant and eel,
But noo-a-days e'en wi' ain's se
At hame it's hard to feel.

Hugh MacDiarmid

ilka: each, every
gowpin': gaping, staring
mell: mix
tit: titmouse
ain's se: oneself

THE SAME OLD LAW

The wild gander leads his flock through the cool night,
Ya-honk he says, and sounds it down to me like an
invitation,
The pert may suppose it meaningless, but I listening close,
Find its purpose and place up there toward the wintry sky.

The sharp-hoof'd moose of the north, the cat on the
house-sill, the chickadee, the prairie-dog,
The litter of the grunting sow as they tug at her teats,
The brood of the turkey-hen and she with her half-spread
wings,
I see in them and myself the same old law.

Walt Whitman

from *Song of Myself*

TO A MOUSE,

On turning her up in her nest with the plough, November 1785

Wee, sleekit, cow'rin, tim'rous beastie,
O, what a panic's in thy breastie!
Thou need na start awa sae hasty,
    Wi' bickering brattle!
I wad be laith to rin an' chase thee,
    Wi' murd'ring pattle!

I'm truly sorry Man's dominion
Has broken Nature's social union,
An' justifies that ill opinion,
    Which makes thee startle,
At me, thy poor, earth-born companion,
    An' fellow-mortal!

I dount na, whyles, but thou may thieve;
What then? poor beastie, thou maun live!
A daimen-icker in a thrave
    'S a sma' request:
I'll get a blessin wi' the lave,
    And never miss't!

Thy wee bit housie, too, in ruin!
Its silly wa's the win's are strewin!
An' naething, now, to big a new ane
    O' foggage green!
An' bleak December's winds ensuin,
    Baith snell an' keen!

Thou saw the fields laid bare an' waste,
An' weary Winter comin fast,
An' cozie here, beneath the blast,
        Thou thought to dwell,–
Till crash! the cruel coulter past,
        Out thro' thy cell.

That wee bit heap o' leaves an' stibble,
Has cost thee mony a weary nibble!
Now thou's turn'd out, for a' thy trouble,
        But house or hald,
To thole the Winter's sleety dribble,
        An' cranreuch cauld!

But Mousie, thou art no thy lane,
In proving foresight may be vain:
The best-laid schemes o' Mice an Men
        Gang aft a-gley,
An' lea'e us nought but grief an' pain,
        For promis'd joy!

Still thou art blest, compar'd wi' me!
The present only toucheth thee:
But Och! I backward cast my e'e
        On prospects drear!
An' forward, tho' I canna see,
        I guess an' fear!

Robert Burns

sleekit: sleek bickering brattle: fast, noisy dash
laith: loath pattle: plough staff whyles: sometimes
a daimen-icker in a thrave: an occasional ear of corn
lave: remainder big: erect, build foggage: moss
snell: bitterly cold coulter: plough-share
but house or hald: without house or holding
thole: bear, suffer dribble: drizzle cranreuch: hoar-frost
no thy lane: not alone a-gley: askew, amiss

TWO GUESTS FROM ALABAMA

Once Paumanok,
When the lilac-scent was in the air and Fifth-month grass was growing,
Up this seashore in some briers,
Two feather'd guests from Alabama, two together,
And their nest, and four light-green eggs spotted with brown,
And every day the he-bird to and fro near at hand,
And every day the she-bird crouch'd on her nest, silent, with bright eyes,
And every day I, a curious boy, never too close, never disturbing them,
Cautiously peering, absorbing, translating.

Shine! shine! shine!
Pour down your warmth, great sun!
While we bask, we two together.

Two together!
Winds blow south, or winds blow north,
Day come white, or night come black,
Home, or rivers and mountains from home,
Singing all time, minding no time,
While we two keep together.

Till of a sudden,
May-be kill'd, unknown to her mate,
One forenoon the she-bird crouch'd not on the nest,
Nor return'd that afternoon, nor the next,
Nor ever appear'd again.

And thenceforward all summer in the sound of the sea,
And at night under the full of the moon in calmer
weather,
Over the hoarse surging of the sea,
Or flitting from brier to brier by day,
I saw, I heard at intervals the remaining one, the
he-bird,
The solitary guest from Alabama.

Blow! blow! blow!
Blow up sea-winds along Paumanok's shore;
I wait and wait till you blow my mate to me.

Walt Whitman

from *Out of the Cradle Endlessly Rocking*

Paumanok: Indian name for Long Island, New York

BUFFALO DUSK

The buffaloes are gone.
And those who saw the buffaloes are gone.
Those who saw the buffaloes by thousands and
    how they pawed the prairie sod into dust
    with their hoofs, their great heads down
    pawing on in a great pageant of dusk,
Those who saw the buffaloes are gone.
And the buffaloes are gone.

Carl Sandburg

BOOK-MOTH

A moth ate a word.   To me it seemed
A marvellous thing   when I learned the wonder
That a worm had swallowed,   in darkness stolen,
The song of a man,   his glorious sayings,
A great man's strength;   and the thieving guest
Was no whit the wiser   for the words it ate.

Anonymous

TRANSLATED FROM OLD ENGLISH BY
Charles W. Kennedy

THE MOUSETRAP

I

Palmström hasn't a crumb in the house;
Nevertheless, he has a mouse.

Von Korf, upset by his friend's distress,
Builds a room out of trellises

And places Palmström there, within,
Fiddling an exquisite violin.

It gets late; the stars shine bright;
Palmström makes music in the night

Till, in the midst of this serenade,
The mouse strolls in to promenade.

Behind it, by some secret trick,
A trap door closes, quiet, quick.

Before it, Palmström, immediately,
Sinks into slumber, silently.

II

Von Korf arrives in the early dawn
And loads this useful invention on

The nearest medium-sized, as it were,
Moving van for furniture,

Which is hauled, then, by a powerful horse,
Nimbly, into the distant forest.

There, profoundly isolated,
This strange couple are liberated;

First the mouse comes strolling out,
And then Palmström, after the mouse.

The animal does not take fright,
But takes to its new home with delight.

Palmström, meanwhile, observing this,
Drives home with Korf, transformed by bliss.

Christian Morgenstern

TRANSLATED FROM THE GERMAN BY
W. D. Snodgrass

DO NOT BELIEVE YOUR SHAKESPEARE'S GRIEF

Do not believe your Shakespeare's grief
Is more than tearing of a leaf.
Tread on an ant, he knows a pain
Cruel and red and broad as Spain.
Starving mice and weeping trees
The hemlock drink with Socrates.
The lark, defeated, knows a loss
As black as hangs upon a cross.

Conrad Aiken

from *The Argument*

THE MEADOW MOUSE

I

In a shoe box stuffed in an old nylon stocking
Sleeps the baby mouse I found in the meadow,
Where he trembled and shook beneath a stick
Till I caught him up by the tail and brought him in,
Cradled in my hand,
A little quaker, the whole body of him trembling,
His absurd whiskers sticking out like a cartoon-mouse,
His feet like small leaves,
Little lizard-feet,
Whitish and spread wide when he tried to struggle away,
Wriggling like a minuscule puppy.

Now he's eaten his three kinds of cheese and drunk from his bottle-cap watering-trough—
So much he just lies in one corner,
His tail curled under him, his belly big
As his head; his bat-like ears
Twitching, tilting toward the least sound.

Do I imagine he no longer trembles
When I come close to him?
He seems no longer to tremble.

II

But this morning the shoe-box house on the back porch is empty.
Where has he gone, my meadow mouse,

My thumb of a child that nuzzled in my palm?—
To run under the hawk's wing,
Under the eye of the great owl watching from the elm-tree,
To live by courtesy of the shrike, the snake, the tom-cat.

I think of the nestling fallen into the deep grass,
The turtle gasping in the dusty rubble of the highway,
The paralytic stunned in the tub, and the water rising,—
All things innocent, hapless, forsaken.

Theodore Roethke

THE FARMER'S GUN

The wood is full of rooks
That by their faded looks
No more on thievery will thrive,
As when they were alive,
Nor fill the air with the hoarse noise
That most of all is England's pleasant voice.

How ugly is this work of man,
Seen in the bald brain-pan,
Voracious bill,
Torn wing, uprooted quill
And host of tiny glistening flies
That lend false lustre to these empty eyes.

More delicate is nature's way
Whereby all creatures know their day,
And hearing Death call, 'Come,
Here is a bone or crumb,'
Bury themselves before they die
And leave no trace of foul mortality.

Andrew Young

VICE VERSA

The rabbit sits upon the green
In the belief it is unseen.

Yet from a neighboring mountain slope
A huntsman with a telescope

Observes the little beast with tense
And silent-watching diligence.

Him also from the distant sky
God holds in his all-seeing eye.

Christian Morgenstern

TRANSLATED FROM THE GERMAN BY
R. F. C. Hull

THE RED COCKATOO

Sent as a present from Annam—
A red cockatoo.
Coloured like the peach-tree blossom,
Speaking with the speech of men.
And they did to it what is always done
To the learned and eloquent.
They took a cage with stout bars
And shut it up inside.

Po Chü-i

TRANSLATED FROM THE CHINESE BY
Arthur Waley

Annam: central Vietnam

THE GIFTS OF THE ANIMALS TO MAN

The lion heart, the ounce gave active might,
The horse good shape, the sparrow lust to play,
Nightingale voice, enticing songs to say;
Elephant gave a perfect memory,
And parrot ready tongue, that to apply.

The fox gave craft, the dog gave flattery,
Ass patience, the mole a working thought,
Eagle high look, wolf secret cruelty,
Monkey sweet breath, the cow her fair eyes brought,
The ermine whitest skin, spotted with naught;
The sheep mild-seeming face, climbing the bear,
The stag did give the harm-eschewing fear.

The hare her sleights, the cat his melancholy,
Ant industry, and cony skill to build;
Cranes order, storks to be appearing holy;
Chameleon ease to change, duck ease to yield;
Crocodile, tears which might be falsely spill'd;
Ape great thing gave, though he did mowing stand,
The instrument of instruments, the hand.

Sir Philip Sidney

from *Shepherd Song*

ounce: kind of wild cat
sleights: cunning tricks
cony: rabbit
mowing: grimacing, mocking

THE MERRY COUNTRY LAD

Who can live in heart so glad
As the merry country lad?
Who upon a fair green balk
May at pleasure sit and walk,
And amid the azure skies
See the morning sun arise,
While he hears in every spring
How the birds do chirp and sing:
Or before the hounds in cry,
See the hare go stealing by:
Or along the shallow brook,
Angling with a baited hook,
See the fishes leap and play
In a blessèd sunny day:
Or to hear the partridge call
Till she have her covey all:
Or to see the subtle fox,
How the villain plies the box:
After feeding on his prey,
How he closely sneaks away,
Through the hedge and down the furrow
Till he gets into his burrow:
Then the bee to gather honey:
And the little black-haired coney,
On a bank for sunny place,
With her forefeet wash her face:

Are not these, with thousands moe
Than the court of kings do know,
The true pleasing spirit's sights
That may breed true love's delights?

Nicholas Breton

from *The Passionate Shepherd*

balk: bank
covey: brood of birds
plies the box: raids the chicken run
coney: rabbit
moe: more

I HEARD A LINNET COURTING

I heard a linnet courting
  His lady in the spring:
His mates were idly sporting,
  Nor stayed to hear him sing
    His song of love.—
I fear my speech distorting
    His tender love.

The phrases of his pleading
  Were full of young delight;
And she that gave him heeding
  Interpreted aright
    His gay, sweet notes,—
So sadly marred in the reading,—
    His tender notes.

And when he ceased, the hearer
  Awaited the refrain,
Till swiftly perching nearer
  He sang his song again,
    His pretty song:—
Would that my verse spake clearer
    His tender song!

Ye happy, airy creatures!
   That in the merry spring
Think not of what misfeatures
   Or cares the year may bring;
      But unto love
Resign your simple natures,
      To tender love.

Robert Bridges

WITH MYRIAD VOICES GRASS WAS FILLED

With myriad voices grass was filled.
A beetle clicked. A cricket shrilled.
A host of ants, deep underground,
Murmured in earth a mournful sound,
Sang slowly, rolling grains of sand.
The scarlet eft, with scarlet hand
Clutching a twig, and small dark eye,
Under an oak-leaf ticked his cry.
And buttercups, like sea-surf swinging,
Their countless gentle gold-bells ringing,
Tinkled for gnats and tolled for bees
And chimed for dragon-flies. Vast trees
Flung down their blossoms green that fell
Roaring through air, each clanging bell
Quenched in the grass. White moth on thistle
Fanned with his wings and made them whistle . . .

Conrad Aiken

from *John Deth*

eft: a small newt

HARES AT PLAY

The birds are gone to bed, the cows are still,
And sheep lie panting on each old mole-hill;
And underneath the willow's grey-green bough,
Like toil a-resting, lies the fallow plough.
The timid hares throw daylight fears away
On the lane's road to dust and dance and play,
Then dabble in the grain by naught deterred
To lick the dew-fall from the barley's beard;
Then out they sturt again and round the hill
Like happy thoughts dance, squat, and loiter still,
Till milking maidens in the early morn
Jingle their yokes and sturt them in the corn;
Through well-known beaten paths each nimbling hare
Sturts quick as fear, and seeks its hidden lair.

John Clare

sturt: to move suddenly, to start

OTTERS

I'll be an otter, and I'll let you swim
A mate beside me; we will venture down
A deep, full river when the sky above
Is shut of the sun; spoilers are we;
Thick-coated; no dog's tooth can bite at our veins–
With ears and eyes of poachers; deep-earthed ones
Turned hunters; let him slip past,
The little vole, my teeth are on an edge
For the King-fish of the River!

I hold him up–
The glittering salmon that smells of the sea;
I hold him up and whistle!

Now we go
Back to our earth; we will tear and eat
Sea-smelling salmon; you will tell the cubs
I am the Booty-bringer: I am the Lord
Of the River–the deep, dark, full, and flowing River!

Padraic Colum

vole: mouse-like quadruped

THE WOOD-WEASEL

emerges daintily, the skunk—
don't laugh—in sylvan black and white chipmunk
regalia. The inky thing
adaptively whited with glistening
goat-fur, is wood-warden. In his
ermined, well-cuttlefish-inked wool, he is
determination's totem. Out-
lawed? His sweet face and powerful feet go about
in chieftain's coat of Chilcat cloth.
He is his own protection from the moth—

noble little warrior. That
otter-skin on it—the living pole-cat—
smothers anything that stings. Well—
this same weasel's playful and his weasel
associates are too. Only
Wood-weasels shall associate with me.

Marianne Moore

totem: emblem, symbol

BOY IN A POND

Was I not muskrat, water-snake, raccoon?
Was I not dragon-fly and diving loon?
Polliwog, dreaming under lily-pads?
Victor of song in frog-olympiads?
Crawfish investigating runes of stone?
Minnow of sucking glass and glassy bone?
I flamed a water-beetle's fat vermilion,
I joined the water-striders' cool cotillion;
I made my body calamus for thin
Silk fish to nibble at me, toe to chin;
And once, while I was floating like a mink,
Straight in my face a doe looked down to drink!
I saw my soul burn in her golden eyes,
Globed among ecstasies!
I caught her breath above a pickerel-bloom:
It was black plum and russet-mild mushroom.

James Whaler

from *Runaway*

runes: letters of an ancient alphabet
calamus: a reed
cotillion: a dance

GRIZZLY

Coward,—of heroic size,
In whose lazy muscles lies
Strength we fear and yet despise;
Savage,—whose relentless tusks
Are content with acorn husks;
Robber,—whose exploits ne'er soared
O'er the bee's or squirrel's hoard;
Whiskered chin and feeble nose,
Claws of steel on baby toes,—
Here, in solitude and shade,
Shambling, shuffling plantigrade,
Be thy courses undismayed!

Here, where Nature makes thy bed,
Let thy rude, half-human tread
    Point to hidden Indian springs,
Lost in ferns and fragrant grasses,
    Hovered o'er by timid wings,
Where the wood-duck lightly passes,
Where the wild bee holds her sweets,—
Epicurean retreats,
Fit for thee, and better than
Fearful spoils of dangerous man.

In thy fat-jowled deviltry
Friar Tuck shall live in thee;
Thou mayest levy tithe and dole;
    Thou shalt spread the woodland cheer,
From the pilgrim taking toll;
    Match thy cunning with his fear;
Eat, and drink, and have thy fill;
Yet remain an outlaw still!

Bret Harte

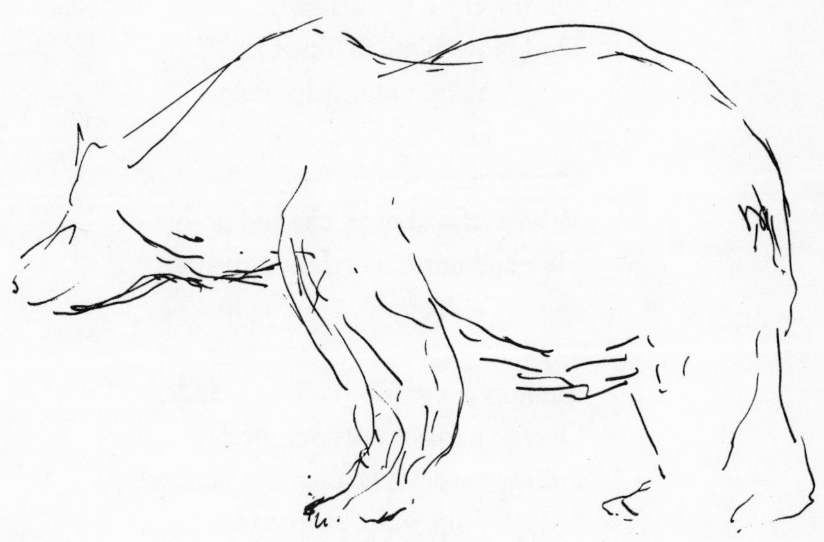

plantigrade: animal that walks on its soles with heels touching the ground

YOLP, YOLP, YOLP, YOLP

Hark! They cry! I hear by that
The dogs have put the hare from quat
Then woe be unto little Wat!
Yolp, yolp, yolp, yolp.

Hollo in the hind dogs, hollo!
So come on then—solla! solla!—
And let us so blithely follow.
Yolp, yolp, yolp, yolp.

Oh, the dogs are out of sight,
But the cry is my delight:
Hark how Jumball hits it right!
Yolp, yolp, yolp, yolp.

Over briars, over bushes!
Who's affeard of pricks and pushes
He's no hunter worth two rushes.
Yolp, yolp, yolp, yolp.

But how long thus shall we wander?
Oh, the hare's a lusty stander!
Follow apace! The dogs are yonder!
Yolp, yolp, yolp, yolp.

Anonymous

quat: squatting
Wat: name given to hares

REYNARD THE FOX

On óld Cold Crendon's windy tops
Grows wintrily Blown Hilcote Copse,
Wind-bitten beech with badger barrows,
Where brocks eat wasp-grubs with their marrows,
And foxes lie on short-grassed turf,
Nose between paws, to hear the surf
Of wind in the beeches drowsily.
There was our fox bred lustily
Three years before, and there he berthed
Under the beech-roots snugly earthed,
With a roof of flint and a floor of chalk
And ten bitten hens' heads each on its stalk,
Some rabbits' paws, some fur from scuts,
A badger's corpse and a smell of guts.
And there on the night before my tale
He trotted out for a point in the vale.
He saw, from the cover edge, the valley
Go trooping down with its droops of sally
To the brimming river's lipping bend,
And a light in the inn at Water's End.
He heard the owl go hunting by
And the shriek of the mouse the owl made die,
And the purr of the owl as he tore the red
Strings from between his claws and fed;
The smack of joy of the horny lips
Marbled green with the blobby strips.
He saw the farms where dogs were barking,
Cold Crendon Court and Copsecote Larking;
The fault with the spring as bright as gleed,
Green-slash-laced with water weed.

A glare in the sky still marked the town,
Though all folk slept and the blinds were down,
The street lamps watched the empty square,
The night-cat sang his evil there.
The fox's nose tipped up and round
Since smell is a part of sight and sound.
Delicate smells were drifting by,
The sharp nose flaired them heedfully;
Patridges in the clover stubble,
Crouched in a ring for the stoat to nubble.
Rabbit bucks beginning to box;

A scratching place for the pheasant cocks;
A hare in the dead grass near the drain,
And another smell like the spring again.

John Masefield

from *Reynard the Fox*

brocks: badgers
scuts: tails
gleed: a live coal, ember

He rises and begins to round,
He drops the silver chain of sound
Of many links without a break,
In chirrup, whistle, slur and shake,
All intervolv'd and spreading wide,
Like water-dimples down a tide
Where ripple ripple overcurls
And eddy into eddy whirls;
A press of hurried notes that run
So fleet they scarce are more than one,
Yet changingly the trills repeat
And linger ringing. . . . .

For singing till his heaven fills,
'Tis love of earth that he instils,
And ever winging up and up,
Our valley is his golden cup,
And he the wine which overflows
To lift us with him as he goes:
The woods and brooks, the sheep and kine
He is, the hills, the human line,
The meadows green, the fallows brown,
The dreams of labor in the town;
He sings the sap, the quicken'd veins;
The wedding song of sun and rains

He is, the dance of children, thanks
Of sowers, shout of primrose-banks,
And eye of violets while they breathe;
All these the circling song will wreathe,
And you shall hear the herb and tree,
The better heart of men shall see,
Shall feel celestially, as long
As you crave nothing save the song.

George Meredith

from *The Lark Ascending*

THE GOAT PATHS

I.

The crooked paths
Go every way
Upon the hill
—They wind about
Through the heather,
In and out
Of a quiet
Sunniness.

And the goats,
Day after day,
Stray
In sunny
Quietness;
Cropping here,
And cropping there
—As they pause,

And turn,
And pass—
Now a bit
Of heather spray,
Now a mouthful
Of the grass.

2

In the deeper
Sunniness;
In the place
Where nothing stirs;
Quietly
In quietness;
In the quiet
Of the furze
They stand a while;
They dream;
They lie;
They stare
Upon the roving sky.

If you approach
They run away!
They will stare,
And stamp,
And bound,
With a sudden angry sound,

To the sunny
Quietude;
To crouch again,
Where nothing stirs,
In the quiet
Of the furze:
To crouch them down again,
And brood,
In the sunny
Solitude.

3

Were I but
As free
As they,
I would stray
Away
And brood;
I would beat
A hidden way,
Through the quiet
Heather spray,
To a sunny
Solitude.

F

And should you come
I'd run away!
I would make an angry sound,
I would stare,
And stamp,
And bound
To the deeper
Quietude;
To the place
Where nothing stirs
In the quiet
Of the furze.

4

In that airy
Quietness
I would dream
As long as they:
Through the quiet
Sunniness
I would stray
Away
And brood,
All among
The heather spray,
In a sunny
Solitude.

—I would think
Until I found
Something
I can never find;
—Something
Lying
On the ground,
In the bottom
Of my mind.

James Stephens

CROW

A hundred autumns he has wheeled
Above this solitary field.
Here he circled after corn
Before the oldest man was born.
When the oldest man is dead
He will be unsurfeited.
See him crouch upon a limb
With his banquet under him.
Hear the echo of his caw
Give the skirting forest law.
Down he drops, and struts among
The rows of supper, tassel-hung.
Not a grain is left behind
That his polished beak can find.
He is full; he rises slow
To watch the evening come and go.
From the barren branch, his rest,
All is open to the west;
And the light along his wing
Is a sleek and oily thing.
Past an island floats the gaze
Of this ancientest of days.

Green and orange and purple dye
Is reflected in his eye.
There is an elm tree in the wood
Where his dwelling place has stood
All the hundreds of his years.
There he sails and disappears.

Mark Van Doren

FIREFLIES IN THE GARDEN

Here come real stars to fill the upper skies,
And here on earth come emulating flies,
That though they never equal stars in size,
(And they were never really stars at heart)
Achieve at times a very star-like start.
Only, of course, they can't sustain the part.

Robert Frost

emulate: imitate

A MARTIAL MOUSE

A mouse, whose martial value has so long
Ago been try'd, and by old Homer sung,
And purchas'd him more everlasting glory
Than all his Grecian and his Trojan story,
Though he appears unequal matcht, I grant,
In bulk and stature by the elephant,
Yet frequently has been observ'd in battle
To have reduc'd the proud and haughty cattle,
When, having boldly enter'd the redoubt,
And storm'd the dreadful outwork of his snout,
The little vermin, like an errant-knight,
Has slain the huge gigantic beast in fight.

Samuel Butler

redoubt: outlying fortification

THE MARRIAGE OF THE FROG AND THE MOUSE

'Twas the Frogge in the well,
  Humble-dum, humble-dum.
And the merrie Mouse in the Mill,
  tweedle tweedle, twino.

The Frogge would a woing ride,
Sword and buckler by his side.

When he was upon his high horse set,
His boots they shone as blacke as jet.

When she came to the merry mill pin,
Lady Mouse been you within?

Then came out the dusty Mouse,
I am the Lady of this house.

Hast thou any minde of me?
I hane e'ne great mind of thee.

Who shall this marriage make?
Our Lord which is the Rat.

What shall we have to our supper?
Three beanes in a pound of butter.

When supper they were at,
The Frog, the Mouse, and even the Rat,

Then came in Gib our Cat
And catcht the Mouse enen by the backe.

Then did they separate,
And the Frog leapt on the floore so flat.

Then came in Dicke our Drake,
And drew the Frogge enen to the lake.

The Rat run up the wall
    humble-dum, humble-dum.
A goodly company, the dieuell goe with all
    tweedle, tweedle, twino.

Anonymous

pin: door latch or handle
dieuell: devil

THE BUNYIP

The water down the rocky wall
Lets fall its shining stair;
The bunyip in the deep green pool
Looks up it to the air.

the kookaburra drank, he says, then shrieked at me with laughter,
I dragged him down in a hairy hand and ate his thighbones after;
My head is bruised with the falling foam, the water blinds my eye,
Yet I will climb that waterfall and walk upon the sky.

The turpentine and stringybark,
The dark red bloodwoods lean
And drop their shadows in the pool
With blue sky in between.

A beast am I, the bunyip says, my voice a drowning cow's.
Yet am I not a singing bird among these waving boughs?
I raise my black and dripping head, I cry a bubbling cry;
For I shall climb the trunks of trees to walk upon the sky.

Gold and red the gum-trees glow,
Yellow gleam the ferns;
The bunyip in the crimson pool
Believes the water burns.

I know the roots of rocks, he says, I know the door of hell;
I ate the abo's daughter once, I know my faults full well;
Yet sunset walks between the trees and sucks the water dry,
And when the whole world's burnt away I'll walk upon the sky.

The little frogs they call like bells,
The bunyip swims alone;
Across the pool the stars are laid
Like stone by silver stone.

What did I do before I was born, the bunyip asks the night;
I looked at myself in the water's glass and I nearly died of fright;
Condemned to haunt a pool in the bush while a thousand years go by—
Yet I walk on the stars like stepping-stones and I'll climb them into the sky.

A lady walks across the night
And sees that mirror there;
Oh, is it for herself alone
The moon lets down her hair?

The yabbie's back is green for her, his claws are
opal-blue,
Look for my soul, the bunyip says, for it was a jewel too.
I bellowed with woe to the yabbie once, but all I said
was a lie,
For I'll catch the moon by her silver hair and dance her
around the sky.

Douglas Stewart

bunyip: fabulous animal in Australian mythology
kookaburra: bird of Australia
abo: short for Aborigine
yabbie: small crayfish

THE EXAMPLE

Here's an example from
  A Butterfly;
That on a rough, hard rock
  Happy can lie;
Friendless and all alone
  On this unsweetened stone.

Now let my bed be hard,
  No care take I;
I'll make my joy like this
  Small Butterfly,
Whose happy heart has power
To make a stone a flower.

W. H. Davies

THE DRAGON-FLY

"To-day I saw the dragon-fly
Come from the wells where he did lie.

"An inner impulse rent the veil
Of his old husk: from head to tail
Came out clear plates of sapphire mail.

"He dried his wings: like gauze they grew;
Thro' crofts and pastures wet with dew
A living flash of light he flew."

Alfred, Lord Tennyson

from *The Two Voices*

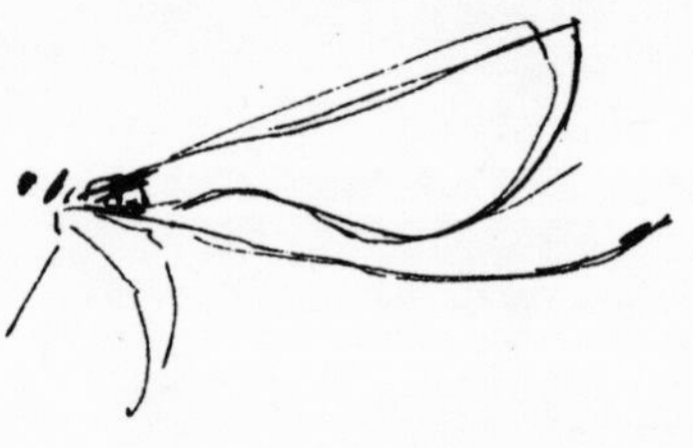

HEN'S NEST

Among the orchard weeds, from every search,
Snugly and sure, the old hen's nest is made,
Who cackles every morning from her perch
To tell the servant girl new eggs are laid;
Who lays her washing by, and far and near
Goes seeking all about from day to day,
And stung with nettles tramples everywhere;
But still the cackling pullet lays away.
The boy on Sundays goes the stack to pull
In hopes to find her there, but naught is seen,
And takes his hat and thinks to find it full,
She's laid so long so many might have been.
But naught is found and all is given o'er
Till the young brood come chirping to the door.

John Clare

stack: haystack

THE COW IN APPLE TIME

Something inspires the only cow of late
To make no more of a wall than an open gate,
And think no more of wall-builders than fools.
Her face is flecked with pomace and she drools
A cider syrup. Having tasted fruit,
She scorns a pasture withering to the root.
She runs from tree to tree where lie and sweeten
The windfalls spiked with stubble and worm-eaten.
She leaves them bitten when she has to fly.
She bellows on a knoll against the sky.
Her udder shrivels and the milk goes dry.

Robert Frost

pomace: crushed apples
windfalls: fallen fruit

NICHOLAS NYE

Thistle and darnel and dock grew there,
And a bush, in the corner, of may,
On the orchard wall I used to sprawl,
In the blazing heat of the day;
Half asleep and half awake,
While the birds went twittering by,
And nobody there my lone to share but Nicholas Nye.

Nicholas Nye was lean and grey,
Lame of leg and old,
More than a score of donkey's years
He had seen since he was foaled;
He munched the thistles, purple and spiked,
Would sometimes stoop and sigh,
And turn his head, as if he said,
"Poor Nicholas Nye!"

Alone with his shadows he'd drowse in the meadow,
   Lazily swinging his tail,
At break of day he used to bray,—
   Not much too hearty and hale;
But a wonderful gumption was under his skin,
   And a clear calm light in his eye,
And once in a while: he'd smile:—
   Would Nicholas Nye.

Seem to be smiling at me, he would,
   From his bush, in the corner, of may—
Bony and ownerless, widowed and worn,
   Knobble-kneed, lonely and grey;
And over the grass would seem to pass
   'Neath the deep dark blue of the sky,
Something much better than words between me
   And Nicholas Nye.

But dusk would come in the apple boughs,
   The green of the glow-worm shine,
The birds in nest would crouch to rest,
   And home I'd trudge to mine;
And there, in the moonlight, dark with dew,
   Asking not wherefore nor why,
Would brood like a ghost, and as still as a post,
   Old Nicholas Nye.

Walter de la Mare

darnel and dock: weeds   may: hawthorn blossom

A TRUEBLUE GENTLEMAN

This gentleman the charming duck
Quack quack says he
My tail's on
Fire, but he's only kidding

You can tell that

By his grin
He's one big grin, from wobbly
Feet to wobbly tail
Quack quack he tells us

Tail's on fire again

Ah yes
This charming gentleman the duck
With
His quaint alarms and
Trick of walking like a
Drunken hat
Quack quack says he

There's your fried egg

Kenneth Patchen

SHEEP

When I was once in Baltimore,
  A man came up to me and cried,
"Come, I have eighteen hundred sheep,
  And we will sail on Tuesday's tide.

"If you will sail with me, young man,
  I'll pay you fifty shillings down;
These eighteen hundred sheep I take
  From Baltimore to Glasgow town."

He paid me fifty shillings down,
  I sailed with eighteen hundred sheep;
We soon had cleared the harbour's mouth,
  We soon were in the salt sea deep.

The first night we were out at sea
  Those sheep were quiet in their mind;
The second night they cried with fear–
  They smelt no pastures in the wind.

They sniffed, poor things, for their green fields,
  They cried so loud I could not sleep;
For fifty thousand shillings down
  I would not sail again with sheep.

W. H. Davies

BAT

On summer eves with wild delight
  We bawled the bat to spy,
Who in the 'I spy' dusky light
  Shrieked loud and flickered by.
And up we knocked our shuttlecocks
  And tried to hit the moon,
And wondered bats should fly so long
  And they come down so soon.

John Clare

from *Childhood*

THE HEDGEHOG

The hedgehog, from his hollow root,
  Sees the wood-moss clear of snow,
And hunts the hedge for fallen fruit—
  Crab, hip, and winter-bitten sloe;
But often check'd by sudden fears,
  As shepherd-dog his haunt espies,
He rolls up in a ball of spears,
  And all his barking rage defies.

John Clare

from *The Shepherd's Calendar*

crab: crabapple
hip: fruit of the rose
sloe: fruit of the blackthorn

OLD BLUE

Old Blue was tough
As steers can be,
He could walk from Texas
To eternity.

Mean eye, mean horn,
Bony as death,
He could walk the coyotes
Out of breath.

Bronze at his nose,
Iron at his tail,
Each year he walked
The Chisholm Trail.

San Antone
To Kansas or bust,
He churned three long states
Into dust.

Eight hundred miles
He led the van,
He wore out wolves,
Dust storms, and man.

He led the longhorns
To the Abilene train,
And he alone
Came home again.

Loyal and true
To the wrong lot,
Old Blue was Judas
Iscariot.

He led his kind
To the floor running red,
To the knife in the throat,
The axe in the head.

Old Blue led steers
To Doomsday flood,
His name is written
In his own blood.

Robert P. Tristram Coffin

THE PEOPLED AIR

Still is the toiling hand of Care:
The panting herds repose:
Yet hark, how thro' the peopled air
The busy murmur glows!
The insect youth are on the wing,
Eager to taste the honied spring,
And float amid the liquid noon:
Some lightly o'er the current skim,
Some shew their gayly-gilded trim
Quick-glancing to the sun.

To Contemplation's sober eye
Such is the race of Man:
And they that creep, and they that fly,
Shall end where they began.
Alike the Busy and the Gay
But flutter thro' life's little day,
In fortune's varying colours drest:
Brush'd by the hand of rough Mischance,
Or chill'd by Age, their airy dance
They leave, in dust to rest.

Methinks I hear, in accents low,
The sportive kind reply:
Poor moralist! and what art thou?
A solitary fly!

Thy Joys no glittering female meets,
No hive hast thou of hoarded sweets,
No painted plumage to display:
On hasty wings thy youth is flown;
Thy sun is set, thy spring is gone–
We frolick, while 'tis May.

Thomas Gray

from *Ode on the Spring*

MIDWIFE CAT

Beyond the fence she hesitates,
    And drops a paw, and tries the dust.
It is a clearing, but she waits
    No longer minute than she must.

Though a dozen foes may dart
    From out the grass, she crouches by;
Then runs to where the silos start
    To heave their shadows far and high.

Here she folds herself and sleeps;
    But in a moment she has put
The dream aside; and now she creeps
    Across the open, foot by foot,

Till at the threshold of a shed
    She smells the water and the corn
Where a sow is on her bed
    And little pigs are being born.

Silently she leaps, and walks
    All night upon a narrow rafter;
Whence at intervals she talks
    Wise to them she watches after.

Mark Van Doren

THE GRACIOUS AND THE GENTLE THING

The three young heifers were at Summer supper
In the cowpen munching new-mown hay,
Their eyes suffused with sweetness of red clover,
It was no time to pass the time of day.
Their chins went side to side, their cheeks were bulging
Indecorously, and they were eating more;
I was a stranger, I had no introduction,
They had never laid eyes on me before.

Yet when I patted each young lady's sleekness,
Each young lady's lips grew bland and still,
She left the hay that sweetened the whole evening
And beamed on me with eyes deep with good will.
She kissed my hand where it lay on the fence-rail
And breathed her sweetness in my smiling face;
She left her supper, turned her slender beauty
Instantly to practice of good grace.

I stood there below the azure evening
With miles of tender thrushes all around
And thought how up and down the land I never
So natural a courtesy had found
As this night in a barnyard with three heifers.
The gracious and the gentle thing to do,
With never any lesson in good manners,
These innocent and courteous creatures knew.

Robert P. Tristram Coffin

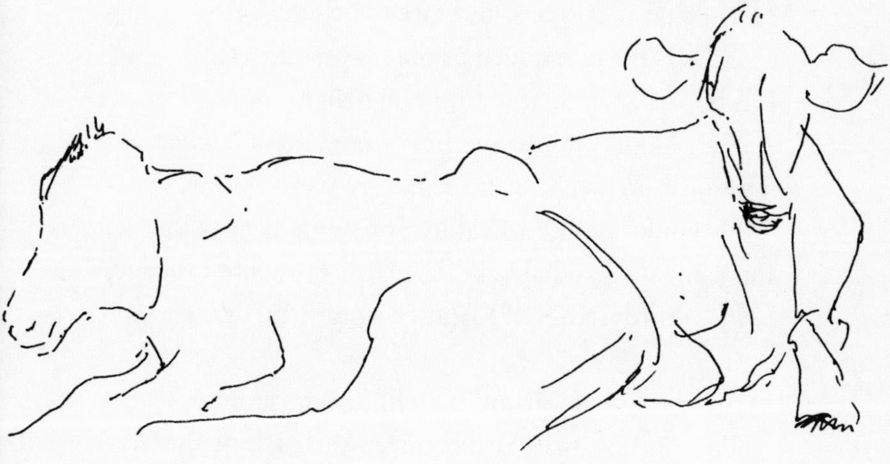

NELL FLAHERTY'S DRAKE

My name it is Nell, right candid I tell,
  And I live near a dell I ne'er will deny,
I had a large drake, the truth for to spake,
  My grandfather left me when going to die;
He was merry and sound, and would weigh twenty pound,
  The universe round would I rove for his sake.
Bad luck to the robber, be he drunken or sober,
  That murdered Nell Flaherty's beautiful drake.

His neck it was green, and rare to be seen,
  He was fit for a queen of the highest degree.
His body so white, it would you delight,
  He was fat, plump, and heavy, and brisk as a bee.
This dear little fellow, his legs they were yellow,
  He could fly like a swallow, or swim like a hake,
But some wicked habbage, to grease his white cabbage,
  Has murdered Nell Flaherty's beautiful drake!

May his pig never grunt, may his cat never hunt,
  That a ghost may him haunt in the dark of the night.
May his hens never lay, may his horse never neigh,
  May his goat fly away like an old paper kite;
May his duck never quack, may his goose be turned black
  And pull down his stack with her long yellow beak.
May the scurvey and itch never part from the britch
  Of the wretch that murdered Nell Flaherty's drake!

May his rooster ne'er crow, may his bellows not blow,
Nor potatoes to grow—may he never have none—
May his cradle not rock, may his chest have no lock,
May his wife have no frock for to shade her backbone.
That the bugs and the fleas may this wicked wretch tease,
And a piercing north breeze make him tremble and shake.
May a four-years'-old bug build a nest in the lug
Of the monster that murdered Nell Flaherty's drake.

May his pipe never smoke, may his tea-pot be broke,
And to add to the joke may his kettle not boil;
May he be poorly fed till the hour he is dead.
May he always be fed on lobscouse and fish oil.
May he swell with the gout till his grinders fall out,
May he roar, howl, and shout with a horrid toothache,
May his temple wear horns and his toes carry corns,
The wretch that murdered Nell Flaherty's drake.

May his dog yelp and howl with both hunger and cold,
May his wife always scold till his brains go astray.
May the curse of each hag, that ever carried a bag,
Light down on the wag till his head it turns gray.

May monkeys still bite him, and mad dogs affright
him,
And every one slight him, asleep or awake.
May wasps ever gnaw him, and jackdaws ever claw
him,
The monster that murdered Nell Flaherty's drake.

But the only good news I have to diffuse,
Is of Peter Hughes and Paddy McCade,
And crooked Ned Manson, and big-nosed Bob
Hanson,
Each one had a grandson of my beautiful drake.
Oh! my bird he has dozens of nephews and cousins,
And one I must have, or my heart it will break.
To keep my mind easy, or else I'll run crazy,
And so ends the song of my beautiful drake.

Anonymous

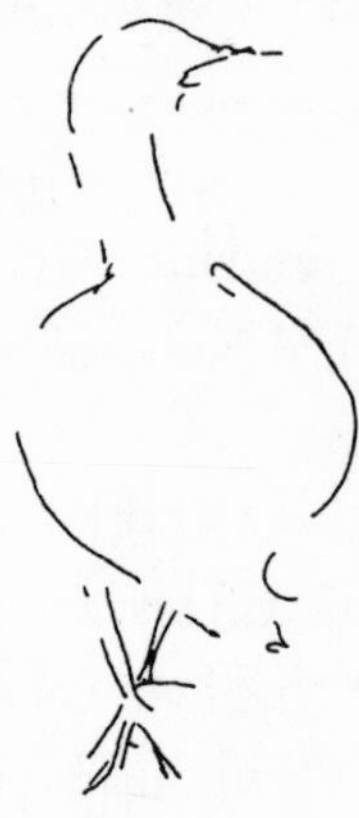

habbage: rough, dishonest, cruel person
lug: ear
lobscouse: a kind of stew

ON THE GRASSHOPPER AND CRICKET

The poetry of earth is never dead:
When all the birds are faint with the hot sun,
And hide in cooling trees, a voice will run
From hedge to hedge about the new-mown mead;
That is the Grasshopper's—he takes the lead
In summer luxury,—he has never done
With his delights; for when tired out with fun
He rests at ease beneath some pleasant weed.
The poetry of earth is ceasing never:
On a lone winter evening, when the frost
Has wrought a silence, from the stove there shrills
The Cricket's song, in warmth increasing ever,
And seems to one in drowsiness half lost,
The Grasshopper's among some grassy hills.

John Keats

THE SATIN MICE CREAKING LAST SUMMER'S GRASS

The satin mice creaking last Summer's grass
Come on dry wine of miraculous clover;
They know; their eyes sprinkle the barn with stars;
They have no history to seal their sharp eyes over.
The pullets on the rafters in the henhouse,
Cockerels, whose eyes see through earth's crust
And track the midnight sun, believe tomorrow
Will strew incredible kernels in their dust.
Only the farmer fumbling, cold and slow,
With his pail and pitchfork does not know.

Every last white-eared sheep in the pen turns amber
At her trusting eyes in the lantern light,
Remembers, without memory, such another
Frosty time and wild wings snowing the night.
The cows know, without knowledge, it once happened,
And happen again in this new barn it may;
Their eyes grow large and tremulous foreseeing
The sun like a gentle daisy in their hay.
Even the milker stroking warm teats half believes
Such things as gods could be on Christmas Eves.

Robert P. Tristram Coffin

FABLE

The mountain and the squirrel
Had a quarrel,
And the former called the latter "Little Prig;"
Bun replied,
"You are doubtless very big;
But all sorts of things and weather
Must be taken in together,
To make up a year
And a sphere.
And I think it no disgrace
To occupy my place.
If I'm not so large as you,
You are not so small as I,
And not half so spry.
I'll not deny you make
A very pretty squirrel track;
Talents differ; all is well and wisely put;
If I cannot carry forests on my back,
Neither can you crack a nut."

Ralph Waldo Emerson

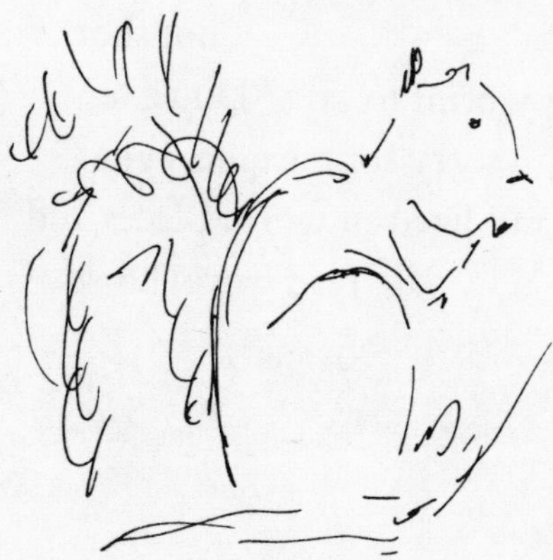

WORMS AND THE WIND

Worms would rather be worms.
Ask a worm and he says, "Who knows what a worm knows?"
Worms go down and up and over and under.
Worms like tunnels.
When worms talk they talk about the worm world.
Worms like it in the dark.
Neither the sun nor the moon interests a worm.
Zigzag worms hate circle worms.
Curve worms never trust square worms.
Worms know what worms want.
Slide worms are suspicious of crawl worms.
One worm asks another, "How does your belly drag today?"
The shape of a crooked worm satisfies a crooked worm.
A straight worm says, "Why not be straight?"
Worms tired of crawling begin to slither.
Long worms slither farther than short worms.
Middle-sized worms say, "It is nice to be neither long nor short."
Old worms teach young worms to say, "Don't be sorry for me unless you
have been a worm and lived in worm places and read worm books."

When worms go to war they dig in, come out and
fight, dig in again,
come out and fight again, dig in again, and so on.
Worms underground never hear the wind overground
and sometimes they
ask, "What is this wind we hear of?"

Carl Sandburg

THE PIG-TALE

There was a Pig that sat alone
  Beside a ruined Pump:
By day and night he made his moan—
It would have stirred a heart of stone
To see him wring his hoofs and groan,
  Because he could not jump.

A certain Camel heard him shout—
  A Camel with a hump.
'Oh, is it Grief, or is it Gout?
What is this bellowing about?'
That Pig replied, with quivering snout,
  'Because I cannot jump!'

That Camel scanned him, dreamy-eyed.
  'Methinks you are too plump.
I never knew a Pig so wide—
That wobbled so from side to side—
Who could, however much he tried,
  Do such a thing as *jump!*

'Yet mark those trees, two miles away,
  All clustered in a clump:
If you could trot there twice a day,
Nor ever pause for rest or play,
In the far future—who can say?—
  You may be fit to jump.'

That Camel passed, and left him there,
  Beside the ruined Pump.
Oh, horrid was that Pig's despair!
His shrieks of anguish filled the air.
He wrung his hoofs, he rent his hair,
  Because he could not jump.

There was a Frog that wandered by—
  A sleek and shining lump:
Inspected him with fishy eye,
And said: 'O Pig, what makes you cry?'
And bitter was that Pig's reply,
  'Because I cannot jump!'

That Frog he grinned a grin of glee,
  And hit his chest a thump.
'O Pig,' he said, 'be ruled by me,
And you shall see what you shall see.
This minute, for a trifling fee,
  I'll teach you how to jump!

'You may be faint from many a fall,
  And bruised by many a bump:
But, if you persevere through all,
And practise first on something small,
Concluding with a ten-foot wall,
  You'll find that you *can* jump!'

That Pig looked up with joyful start:
   'Oh, Frog, you *are* a trump!
Your words have healed my inward smart—
Come, name your fee and do your part:
Bring comfort to a broken heart,
   By teaching me to jump!'

'My fee shall be a mutton-chop,
   My goal this ruined Pump.
Observe with what an airy flop
I plant myself upon the top!
Now bend your knees and take a hop,
   For that's the way to jump!'

Uprose that Pig, and rushed, full whack,
   Against the ruined Pump:
Rolled over like an empty sack,
And settled down upon his back,
While all his bones at once went 'Crack!'
   It was a fatal jump.

That Camel passed, as Day grew dim
   Around the ruined Pump.
'O broken heart! O broken limb!
It needs,' that Camel said to him,
'Something more fairy-like and slim,
   To execute a jump!'

That Pig lay still as any stone,
And could not stir a stump:
Nor ever, if the truth were known,
Was he again observed to moan,
Nor ever wring his hoofs and groan,
Because he could not jump.

That Frog made no remark, for he
Was dismal as a dump:
He knew the consequence must be
That he would never get his fee—
And still he sits, in miserie,
Upon that ruined Pump!

Lewis Carroll

OF THE MEAN AND SURE ESTATE

My mother's maids, when they did sew and spin,
They sang sometime a song of the field mouse,
That for because her livelood was but thin

Would needs go seek her townish sister's house.
She thought herself endured to much pain:
The stormy blasts her cave so sore did souse

That when the furrows swimmed with the rain
She must lie cold and wet in sorry plight,
And, worse than that, bare meat there did remain

To comfort her when she her house had dight:
Sometime a barleycorn, sometime a bean,
For which she laboured hard both day and night

In harvest time, whilst she might go and glean.
And when her store was stroyèd with the flood,
Then well away! for she undone was clean.

Then was she fain to take, instead of food,
Sleep if she might, her hunger to beguile.
'My sister' quoth she 'hath a living good,

'And hence from me she dwelleth not a mile.
In cold and storm she lieth warm and dry
In bed of down, and dirt doth not defile

'Her tender foot, she laboureth not as I.
Richly she feedeth and at the rich man's cost,
And for her meat she needs not crave nor cry.

'By sea, by land, of the delicates the most
Her cater seeks and spareth for no peril.
She feedeth on boiled, baken meat, and roast,

'And hath thereof neither charge nor travail.
And, when she list, the liquor of the grape
Doth goad her heart till that her belly swell.'

And at this journey she maketh but a jape:
So forth she goeth, trusting of all this wealth
With her sister her part so to shape

That, if she might keep herself in health,
To live a lady while her health doth last.
And to the door now she is come by stealth,

And with her foot anon she scrapeth full fast.
The other for fear durst not well scarce appear,
Of every noise so was the wretch aghast.

At last she asked softly who was there,
And in her language, as well as she could,
'Peep,' quoth the other. 'Sister, I am here.'

'Peace,' quoth the town mouse, 'why speakest thou so loud?'
And by the hand she took her fair and well.
'Welcome,' quoth she, 'my sister, by the rood.'

She feasted her that joy it was to tell
The fare they had; they drank the wine so clear;
And as to purpose now and then it fell

She cheered her with: 'How, sister, what cheer?'
Amids this joy there fell a sorry chance,
That, wellaway! the stranger bought full dear

The fare she had, For as she looks, askance,
Under a stool she spied two steaming eyes
In a round head with sharp ears. In France

Was never mouse so feared, for though the unwise
Had not yseen such a beast before,
Yet had nature taught her after her guise

To know her foe and dread him evermore.
The town mouse fled; she knew whither to go.
The other had no shift, but wondrous sore

Feared of her life at home she wished her tho.
And to the door, alas, as she did skip
(Th' heaven it would, lo, and eke her chance was so)

At the threshold her sely foot did trip,
And ere she might recover it again
The traitor cat had caught her by the hip

And made her there against her will remain
That had forgotten her poor surety, and rest,
For seeming wealth wherein she thought to reign.

Sir Thomas Wyatt

from *Of the Mean and Sure Estate*

souse: drench, soak   dight: put in order, repaired
cater: buyer of provisions   jape: jest
rood: the cross of Christ   sely: poor, helpless

Of all the birds that I do know
  Philip my Sparrow hath no peer;
For sit she high or lie she low,
  Be she far off, or be she near,
There is no bird so fair, so fine,
Nor yet so fresh as this of mine.

Come in a morning merrily
  When Philip hath been lately fed,
Or in an evening soberly
  When Philip list to go to bed;
It is a heaven to hear my Phip
How she can chirp with cherry lip.

She never wanders far abroad,
  But is at hand when I do call,
If I command she lays on lode
  With lips, with teeth, with tongue and all;
She chants, she chirps, she makes such cheer,
That I believe she hath no peer.

And yet beside all this good sport
  My Philip both can sing and dance,
With new found toys of sundry sort
  My Philip can both prick and prance;
And if you say but "fend cut Phip"
Lord! how the peat will turn and skip!

Her feathers are so fresh of hue
    And so well provèd every day,
So lacks no oil, I warrant you,
    To trim her tail both trick and gay;
And though her mouth be somewhat wide,
Her tongue is sweet and short beside.

And for the rest I dare compare
    She is both tender, sweet and soft;
She never lacketh dainty fare,
    But is well fed, and feedeth oft;
For if my Phip have best to eat,
I warrant you, Phip lacks no meat.

And then if that her meat be good
    And such as like do love alway,
She will lay lips thereon, by rood!
    And see that none be cast away;
For when she once hath felt a fit,
Philip will cry still, "Yet, yet, yet!"

And to tell truth, he were to blame
    Which had so fine a bird as she,
To make him all this goodly game
    Without suspect or jealousy;
He were a churl and knew no good
Would see her faint for lack of food.

Wherefore I sing, and ever shall,
    To praise as I have often proved,
There is no bird amongst them all
    So worthy for to be beloved.
Let others praise what bird they will,
Sweet Philip shall be my bird still.

George Gascoigne

list: desires, wishes to
fend cut: fencing term
peat: term of endearment
proved: turned out

THE CURSING OF THE CAT

That vengeance I ask and cry,
By way of exclamation,
On all the whole nation
Of cats wild and tame;
God send them sorrow and shame!
That cat specially
That slew so cruelly
My little pretty sparrow
That I brought up at Carow.

O cat of carlish kind,
The finde was in thy mind
When thou my bird untwined!
I would thou haddest been blind!
The leopards savage,
The lions in their rage,
Might catch thee in their paws,
And gnaw thee in their jaws!
The serpentes of Libany
Might sting thee venomously!
The dragons with their tongues
Might poison thy liver and lungs!
The manticors of the mountains
Might feed them on thy brains! . . . .

Of Inde the greedy gripes
Might tear out all thy tripes!
Of Arcady the bears
Might pluck away thine ears!

The wild wolf Lycaon
Bite asunder thy backbone!
Of Etna the brenning hill,
That day and night brenneth still,
Set in thy tail a blaze,
That all the world may gaze
And wonder upon thee,
From Ocean the great sea
Unto the Isles of Orcady,
From Tilbury ferry
To the plain of Salísbury
So traitorously my bird to kill
That never ought thee evil will! . . .

John Skelton

from *Phylip Sparrow*

carlish: churlish finde: fiend Libany: Libya
manticor: a fabulous beast gripes: griffins or vultures
Lycaon: a king of Arcadia who was transformed into a wolf
ought: owed brenning: burning

ON A SPANIEL, CALLED BEAU, KILLING A YOUNG BIRD

A spaniel, Beau, that fares like you,
  Well fed, and at his ease,
Should wiser be than to pursue
  Each trifle that he sees.

But you have kill'd a tiny bird,
  Which flew not till to-day,
Against my orders, whom you heard
  Forbidding you the prey.

Nor did you kill that you might eat
  And ease a doggish pain,
For him, though chased with furious heat,
  You left where he was slain.

Nor was he of the thievish sort,
  Or one whom blood allures,
But innocence was all his sport
  Whom you have torn for yours.

My dog! what remedy remains,
  Since teach you all I can,
I see you, after all my pains,
  So much resemble man?

William Cowper

BEAU'S REPLY

Sir, when I flew to seize the bird
  In spite of your command,
A louder voice than yours I heard,
  And harder to withstand.

You cried—Forbear!—but in my breast
  A mightier cried—Proceed!
'Twas nature, Sir, whose strong behest
  Impell'd me to the deed.

Yet, much as nature I respect,
  I ventured once to break
(As you perhaps may recollect)
  Her precept for your sake;

And when your linnet on a day,
  Passing his prison door,
Had flutter'd all his strength away,
  And panting press'd the floor,

Well knowing him a sacred thing,
  Not destined to my tooth,
I only kiss'd his ruffled wing,
  And lick'd the feathers smooth.

Let my obedience then excuse
  My disobedience now,
Nor some reproof yourself refuse
  From your aggrieved bow-wow:

If killing birds be such a crime,
  (Which I can hardly see,)
What think you, Sir, of killing time
  With verse address'd to me!

William Cowper

THE MONK AND HIS CAT

I and Pangur Ban, my cat,
'Tis a like task we are at;
Hunting mice is his delight,
Hunting words I sit all night.

Better far than praise of men
'Tis to sit with book and pen;
Pangur bears me no ill will,
He too plies his simple skill.

'Tis a merry thing to see
At our tasks how glad are we,
When at home we sit and find
Entertainment to our mind.

Oftentimes a mouse will stray
In the hero Pangur's way;
Oftentimes my keen thought set
Takes a meaning in its net.

'Gainst the wall he sets his eye
Full and fierce and sharp and sly;
'Gainst the wall of knowledge I
All my little wisdom try.

When a mouse darts from its den,
O how glad is Pangur then!
O what gladness do I prove
When I solve the doubts I love!

So in peace our tasks we ply,
Pangur Ban, my cat and I;
In our arts we find our bliss,
I have mine and he has his.

Practice every day has made
Pangur perfect in his trade;
I get wisdom day and night
Turning darkness into light.

Anonymous

TRANSLATED FROM THE GAELIC BY
Robin Flower

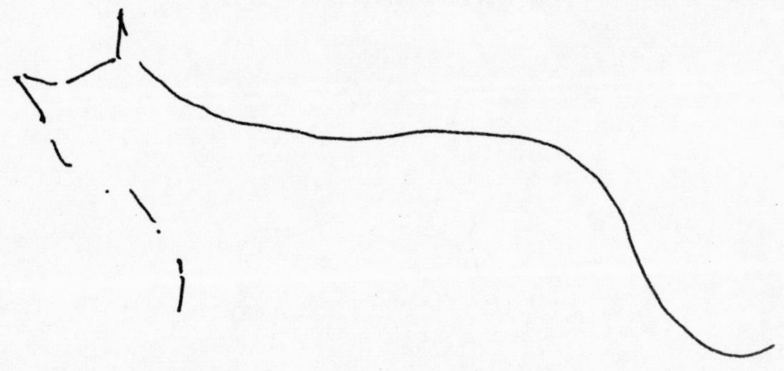

BRAVE ROVER

Rover killed the goat,
He bit him through the throat,
And when it all was over
The goat's ghost haunted Rover.

And yet (the plot here thickens)
Rover killed the chickens.
They thought he was a fox–
And then he killed the cocks.

And now events moved faster:
Rover killed his master,
And then he took the life
Of his late master's wife.

And we must not forget he
Killed Rachel and killed Bettie,
Then Billie and then John.
How dogs do carry on!

To Bradford he repaired.
His great white teeth he bared
And then, with awful snarls,
Polished off Uncle Charles.

Albert in London trembled—
An aspen he resembled—
His life he held not cheap
And wept. (I heard him weep.)

Brave Rover heard him too.
He knew full well who's who,
And entered with a grin
The Fields of Lincoln's Inn.

The Elysian Fields begin
Near those of Lincoln's Inn.
'Tis there that Albert's gone.
How dogs do carry on!

Max Beerbohm

Lincoln's Inn: law buildings in London
Elysian Fields: paradise in Greek mythology

EPITAPH ON LADY OSSORY'S BULLFINCH

All flesh is grass and so are feathers too:
Finches must die as well as I or you.
Beneath a damask rose in good old age
Here lies the tenant of a noble cage.
For forty moons he charmed his lady's ear
And piped obedient oft as she drew near,
Though now stretched out upon a clay-cold bier.
But when the last shrill flageolet shall sound
And raise all dicky-birds from holy ground
This little corpse again its wings shall prune
And sing eternally the selfsame tune
From everlasting night to everlasting noon.

Horace Walpole

flageolet: instrument like a flute
dicky-bird: small bird

THE GARDENER AND THE MOLE

A gardener had watcht a mole
And caught it coming from its hole.
'Mischievous beast!' he cried, 'to harm
The garden as thou dost the farm.
Here thou hast had thy wicked will
Upon my tulip and jonquil.
Behold them drooping and half dead
Upon this torn and tumbled bed.'
  The mole said meekly in reply,
'My star is more to blame than I.
To undermine is mole's commission,
Our house still holds it from tradition.
What lies the nearest us is ours
Decreed so by the higher Powers.
We hear of conies and of hares.
But when commit we deeds like theirs?
We never touch the flowers that blow,
And only bulbs that lurk below.
'Tis true, where we have run, the ground
Is rais'd a trifle, nor quite sound,
Yet, after a few days of rain,
Level and firm it lies again;
Wise men, like you, will rather wait
For these than argue against fate,
Or quarrel with us moles because
We simply follow Nature's laws.
We raise the turf to keep us warm,
Surely in this there is no harm.

Ye break it up to set thereon
A fortress or perhaps a throne,
And pray that God cast down his eyes
Benignly on burnt sacrifice,
The sacrifice of flesh and bone
Fashioned, they tell us, like His own,
Ye in the cold lie all the night
Under thin tents, at morn to fight.
Neither for horn'd nor fleecy cattle,
Start we to mingle in the battle,
Or in the pasture shed their blood
To pamper idleness with food.
Indeed we do eat worms; what then?
Do not those very worms eat men,
And have the impudence to say
Ye shall ere long be such as they?
We never kill or wound a brother,
Men kill by thousands one another,
And, though ye swear ye wish but peace,
Your feuds and warfares never cease.'
Such homebrought truths the gardener,
Though mild by nature, could not bear,
And lest the mole might more have said
He chopt its head off with the spade.

Walter Savage Landor

THE HUNTING TRIBES OF AIR AND EARTH

The hunting tribes of air and earth
Respect the brethren of their birth;
Nature, who loves the claim of kind,
Less cruel chase to each assign'd.
The falcon, poised on soaring wing,
Watches the wild-duck by the spring;
The slow-hound wakes the fox's lair;
The greyhound presses on the hare;
The eagle pounces on the lamb;
The wolf devours the fleecy dam:
Even tiger fell, and sullen bear,
Their likeness and their lineage spare:
Man, only, mars kind Nature's plan,
And turns the fierce pursuit on man,
Plying war's desultory trade,
Incursion, flight, and ambuscade,
Since Nimrod, Cush's mighty son,
At first the bloody game begun.

Sir Walter Scott

from *Rokeby*

Nimrod: a mighty hunter

THE TIGER

Tiger! Tiger! burning bright
In the forests of the night,
What immortal hand or eye
Could frame thy fearful symmetry?

In what distant deeps or skies
Burnt the fire of thine eyes?
On what wings dare he aspire?
What the hand dare seize the fire?

And what shoulder, and what art,
Could twist the sinews of thy heart?
And when thy heart began to beat,
What dread hand? and what dread feet?

What the hammer? what the chain?
In what furnace was thy brain?
What the anvil? what dread grasp
Dare its deadly terrors clasp?

When the stars threw down their spears,
And water'd heaven with their tears,
Did he smile his work to see?
Did he who made the Lamb make thee?

Tiger! Tiger! burning bright
In the forests of the night,
What immortal hand or eye,
Dare frame thy fearful symmetry?

William Blake

THE LION'S SKELETON

How long, O lion, hast thou fleshless lain?
What rapt thy fierce and thirsty eyes away?
First came the vulture: worms, heat, wind, and rain
Ensued, and ardors of the tropic day.
I know not—if they spared it thee—how long
The canker sate within thy monstrous mane,
Till it fell piecemeal and bestrew'd the plain;
Or, shredded by the storming sands, was flung
Again to earth; but now thine ample front,
Whereon the great frowns gather'd, is laid bare;
The thunders of thy throat, which erst were wont
To scare the desert, are no longer there;
The claws remain, but worms, wind, rain, and heat
Have sifted out the substance of thy feet.

Charles Tennyson Turner

THE PANTHER

His weary glance, from passing by the bars,
Has grown into a dazed and vacant stare;
It seems to him there are a thousand bars
And out beyond those bars the empty air.

The pad of his strong feet, that ceaseless sound
Of supple tread behind the iron bands,
Is like a dance of strength circling around,
While in the circle, stunned, a great will stands,

But there are times the pupils of his eyes
Dilate, the strong limbs stand alert, apart,
Tense with the flood of visions that arise
Only to sink and die within his heart.

Rainer Maria Rilke

TRANSLATED FROM THE GERMAN BY
Jessie Lemont

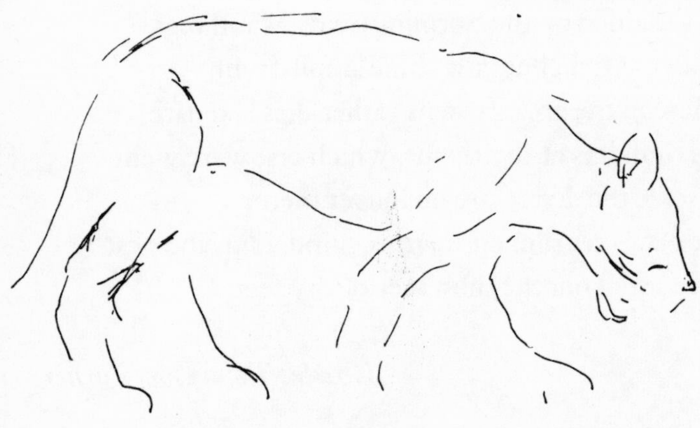

ERIN (ELEPHANT)

Elephant who brings death.
Elephant, a spirit in the bush.
With his single hand
He can pull two palm trees to the ground.
If he had two hands
He would tear the heavens like an old rag.
The spirit who eats dog,
The spirit who eats ram,
The spirit who eats
A whole palm fruit with its thorns.
With his four mortal legs
He tramples down the grass.
Wherever he walks,
The grass is forbidden to stand up again.
An elephant is not a load for an old man—
Nor for a young man either.

Anonymous

TRANSLATED FROM THE YORUBA BY
Ulli Beier

K

THE BULL

See an old unhappy bull,
Sick in soul and body both,
Slouching in the undergrowth
Of the forest beautiful,
Banished from the herd he led,
Bulls and cows a thousand head.

Cranes and gaudy parrots go
Up and down the burning sky;
Tree-top cats purr drowsily
In the dim-day green below;
And troops of monkeys, nutting, some,
All disputing, go and come;

And things abominable sit
Picking offal buck or swine,
On the mess and over it
Burnished flies and beetles shine,
And spiders big as bladders lie
Under hemlocks ten foot high;

And a dotted serpent curled
Round and round and round a tree,
Yellowing its greenery,
Keeps a watch on all the world,
All the world and this old bull
In the forest beautiful.

Bravely by his fall he came:
One he led, a bull of blood
Newly come to lustihood,
Fought and put his prince to shame,
Snuffed and pawed the prostrate head
Tameless even while it bled.

There they left him, every one,
Left him there without a lick,
Left him for the birds to pick,
Left him there for carrion,
Vilely from their bosom cast
Wisdom, worth and love at last.

When the lion left his lair
And roared his beauty through the hills,
And the vultures pecked their quills
And flew into the middle air,
Then this prince no more to reign
Came to life and lived again.

He snuffed the herd in far retreat,
He saw the blood upon the ground,
And snuffed the burning airs around
Still with beevish odours sweet,
While the blood ran down his head
And his mouth ran slaver red.

Pity him, this fallen chief,
All his splendour, all his strength,
All his body's breadth and length
Dwindled down with shame and grief,
Half the bull he was before,
Bones and leather, nothing more.

See him standing dewlap-deep
In the rushes at the lake,
Surly, stupid, half asleep,
Waiting for his heart to break
And the birds to join the flies
Feasting at his bloodshot eyes;

Standing with his head hung down
In a stupor, dreaming things:
Green savannas, jungles brown,
Battlefields and bellowings,
Bulls undone and lions dead
And vultures flapping overhead.

Ralph Hodgson

from *The Bull*

beevish: adjective for beef, oxen

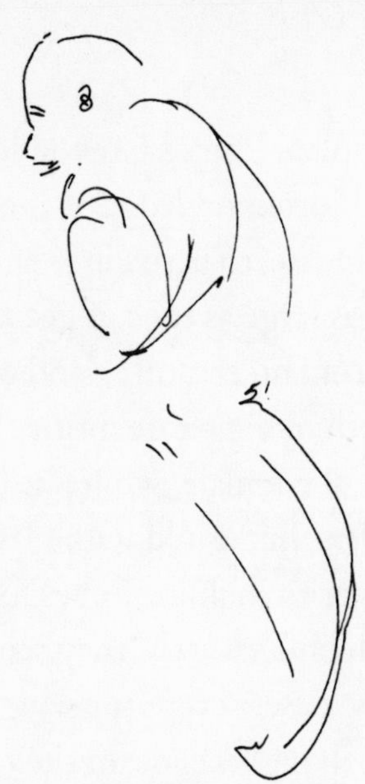

MONKEYS

How ran lithe monkeys through the leaves!
How rush'd they through, brown clad and blue,
Like shuttles hurried through and through
The threads a hasty weaver weaves!
How quick they cast us fruits of gold,
Then loosened hand and all foothold,
And hung, limp, limber, as if dead,
Hung low and listless overhead;
And all the time with half-oped eyes
Bent full on us in mute surprise–
Looked wisely too, as wise hens do
That watch you with the head askew.

Joaquin Miller

from *Walker in Nicaragua*

Contemplate Pliny's Crocodile
that had foreknowledge of the Nile
its yearly rise, to hatch in peace
its eggs as large as eggs of geese
wherefrom no creature, land or sea,
"groweth to bigger quantitie."
Thus of the female, while the male,
tongueless, but arm'd with claw and scale,
his "never twinckling" eyes fixed grimly,
(though underwater "they see dimlie,")
upon the desert crept for slaughter
all day; all night, beneath the water. . . .

The Trochilus, a tiny bird,
did cleanse their jaws of meat and curd,
yet, by sharp thorns upon its head,
obstruct that Crocodile be fed
ingratefully upon its friend!
Natheless this bird its time would spend
in friendly office almost human
preventing entrance of Ichneumon
into vast Crocodile's great maw,
sun-drowsed as he deep breath would draw
in slumber. For this Pharaoh's Mouse
would then, like thief invading house,
steal down his throat and burst his heart
by preying on each vital part,

whereat the dragon, wallowing deep,
would with great mourning sigh and weep,
and roll and toss and throb beneath
those unpacificable teeth
that scored like doom and fire, I tell ye,
with fell Ichneumon in his belly!

William Rose Benét

from *The Bestiary*

THE LAW OF THE JUNGLE

Now this is the Law of the Jungle—as old and as true as the sky;
And the Wolf that shall keep it may prosper, but the Wolf that shall break it must die.

As the creeper that girdles the tree-trunk the Law runneth foreward and back—
For the strength of the Pack is the Wolf, and the strength of the Wolf is the pack.

Wash daily from nose-tip to tail-tip; drink deeply, but never too deep;
And remember the night is for hunting, and forget not the day is for sleep.

The Jackal may follow the Tiger, but, Cub, when thy whiskers are grown,
Remember the Wolf is a hunter—go forth and get food of thine own.

Keep peace with the Lords of the Jungle—the Tiger, the Panther, the Bear;
And trouble not Hathi the Silent, and mock not the Boar in his lair.

When Pack meets with Pack in the Jungle, and neither will go from the trail,
Lie down till the leaders have spoken—it may be fair words shall prevail.

When ye fight with a Wolf of the Pack, ye must fight him alone and afar,
Lest others take part in the quarrel, and the Pack be diminished by war.

The Lair of the Wolf is his refuge, and where he has made him his home,
Not even the Head Wolf may enter, not even the Council may come.

The Lair of the Wolf is his refuge, but where he has digged it too plain,
The Council shall send him a message, and so he shall change it again.

If ye kill before midnight, be silent, and wake not the woods with your bay,
Lest ye frighten the deer from the crops, and the brothers go empty away.

Ye may kill for yourselves, and your mates, and your cubs as they need, and ye can;
But kill not for pleasure of killing, and *seven times never kill Man!*

If ye plunder his Kill from a weaker, devour not all in thy pride;
Pack-Right is the right of the meanest; so leave him the head and the hide.

The Kill of the Pack is the meat of the Pack. Ye must eat where it lies;
And no one may carry away of that meat to his lair, or he dies.

The Kill of the Wolf is the meat of the Wolf. He may do what he will,
But, till he has given permission, the Pack may not eat of that Kill.

Cub-Right is the right of the Yearling. From all of his Pack he may claim
Full-gorge when the killer has eaten; and none may refuse him the same.

Lair-right is the right of the Mother. From all of her year she may claim
One haunch of each kill for her litter; and none may deny her the same.
Cave-Right is the right of the Father—to hunt by himself for his own:
He is freed of all calls to the Pack; he is judged by the Council alone.

Because of his age and his cunning, because of his gripe and
his paw,
In all that the Law leaveth open, the word of the Head
Wolf is Law.

Now these are the Laws of the Jungle, and many and
mighty are they;
But the head and the hoof of the Law and the haunch and
the hump is—Obey!

Rudyard Kipling

Hathi: an elephant

THE SHEPHERD'S DOG AND THE WOLF

A Wolf, with hunger fierce and bold,
Ravaged the plains, and thinned the fold:
Deep in the wood secure he lay,
The thefts of night regaled the day.
In vain the shepherd's wakeful care
Had spread the toils, and watched the snare:
In vain the dog pursued his pace,
The fleeter robber mock'd the chase.
    As Lightfoot ranged the forest round,
By chance his foe's retreat he found.
    'Let us awhile the war suspend,
And reason as from friend to friend.'
'A truce?' replies the Wolf. 'Tis done.
The Dog the parley thus begun:
    'How can that strong intrepid mind
Attack a weak defenceless kind?
Those jaws should prey on nobler food,
And drink the boar's and lion's blood;
Great souls with generous pity melt,
Which coward tyrants never felt.
How harmless is our fleecy care!
Be brave, and let thy mercy spare.'
    'Friend,' says the Wolf, 'the matter weigh;
Nature designed us beasts of prey;
As such, when hunger finds a treat,
'Tis necessary wolves should eat.

If, mindful of the bleating weal,
Thy bosom burn with real zeal;
Hence, and thy tyrant lord beseech;
To him repeat the moving speech:
A Wolf eats sheep but now and then,
Ten thousands are devoured by men.
An open foe may prove a curse,
But pretended friend is worse.'

John Gay

OUT OF THE ARK'S GRIM HOLD

Out of the Ark's grim hold
A torrent of splendour rolled—
From the hollow resounding sides,
Flashing and glittering, came
Panthers with sparkled hides,
And tigers scribbled with flame,
And lions in grisly trains
Cascading their golden manes.
They ramped in the morning light,
And over their stripes and stars
The sun-hot lightnings, quivering bright,
Rippled in zigzag bars.
The wildebeest frisked with the gale
On the crags of a hunchback mountain,
With his heels in the clouds, he flirted his tail
Like the jet of a silvery fountain.
Frail oribi sailed with their golden-skinned
And feathery limbs laid light on the wind.
And the springbok bounced, and fluttered, and flew,
Hooping their spines on the gaunt karroo.
Gay zebras pranced and snorted aloud—
With the crackle of hail their hard hoofs pelt,
And thunder breaks from the rolling cloud
That they raise on the dusty Veld.

O, hark how the rapids of the Congo
Are chanting their rolling strains,
And the sun-dappled herds a-skipping to the song, go
Kicking up the dust on the great, grey plains—
Tsessebe, Koodoo, Buffalo, Bongo,
With the fierce wind foaming in their manes.

Roy Campbell

from *The Flaming Terrapin*

karoo: dry table land in South Africa
Veld: open pasture land in South Africa
tsessebe, koodoo, bongo: kinds of antelopes

A NARROW FELLOW IN THE GRASS

A narrow fellow in the grass
Occasionally rides;
You may have met him,—did you not?
His notice sudden is.

The grass divides as with a comb,
A spotted shaft is seen;
And then it closes at your feet
And opens further on.

He likes a boggy acre,
A floor too cool for corn.
Yet when a child, and barefoot,
I more than once, at morn,

Have passed, I thought, a whip-lash
Unbraiding in the sun,—
When, stooping to secure it,
It wrinkled, and was gone.

Several of nature's people
I know, and they know me;
I feel for them a transport
Of cordiality;

But never met this fellow,
Attended or alone,
Without a tighter breathing,
And zero at the bone.

Emily Dickinson

SNAKE

I saw a young snake glide
Out of the mottled shade
And hang, limp on a stone:
A thin mouth, and a tongue
Stayed, in the still air.

It turned; it drew away;
Its shadow bent in half;
It quickened, and was gone.

I felt my slow blood warm.
I longed to be that thing,
The pure, sensuous form.

And I may be, some time.

Theodore Roethke

KANGAROO

In the northern hemisphere
Life seems to leap at the air, or skim under the wind
Like stags on rocky ground, or pawing horses, or springy scut-tailed rabbits.

Or else rush horizontal to charge at the sky's horizon,
Like bulls or bisons or wild pigs.

Or slip like water slippery toward its ends,
As foxes, stoats, and wolves, and prairie dogs.

Only mice, and moles, and rats, and badgers, and beavers, and perhaps bears
Seem belly-plumbed to the earth's mid-navel.
Or frogs that when they leap come flop, and flop to the centre of the earth.

But the yellow antipodal Kangaroo, when she sits up,
Who can unseat her, like a liquid drop that is heavy, and just touches earth.

The downward drip
The down-urge.
So much denser than cold-blooded frogs.

Delicate mother Kangaroo
Sitting up there rabbit-wise, but huge, plumb-weighted,
And lifting her beautiful slender face, oh! so much more gently and finely lined than a rabbit's, or than a hare's,
Lifting her face to nibble at a round white peppermint drop which she loves, sensitive mother Kangaroo.

Her sensitive, long, pure-bred face.
Her full antipodal eyes, so dark,
So big and quiet and remote, having watched so many empty dawns in silent Australia.

Her little loose hands, and drooping Victorian shoulders.
And then her great weight below the waist, her vast pale belly
With a thin young yellow little paw hanging out, and straggle of a long thin ear, like ribbon,
Like a funny trimming to the middle of her belly, thin little dangle of an immature paw, and one thin ear.

Her belly, her big haunches
And, in addition, the great muscular python-stretch of her tail.

There, she shan't have any more peppermint drops.
So she wistfully, sensitively sniffs the air, and then turns, goes off in slow sad leaps

On the long flat skis of her legs,
Steered and propelled by that steel-strong snake of a tail.

Stops again, half turns, inquisitive to look back.
While something stirs quickly in her belly, and a lean little face comes out, as from a window,

Peaked and a bit dismayed,
Only to disappear again quickly away from the sight of the world, to snuggle down in the warmth,
Leaving the trail of a different paw hanging out.

Still she watches with eternal, cocked wistfulness!
How full her eye are, like the full, fathomless, shining eyes of an Australian black-boy
Who has been lost so many centuries on the margins of existence!

She watches with insatiable wistfulness.
Untold centuries of watching for something to come,
For a new signal from life, in that silent lost land of the South.

Where nothing bites but insects and snakes and the sun, small life.
Where no bull roared, no cow ever lowed, no stag cried, no leopard screeched, no lion coughed, no dog barked,
But all was silent save for parrots occasionally, in the haunted blue bush.

Wistfully watching, with wonderful liquid eyes.
And her weight, all her blood, dripping sack-wise down
towards the earth's centre,
And the live little-one taking its paw at the door of her
belly.

Leap then, and come down on the line that draws to the
earth's deep, heavy centre.

D. H. Lawrence

antipodal: situated on the opposite side of the globe

A RABBIT AS KING OF THE GHOSTS

The difficulty to think at the end of the day,
When the shapeless shadow covers the sun
And nothing is left except light on your fur—

There was the cat slopping its milk all day,
Fat cat, red tongue, green mind, white milk
And August the most peaceful month.

To be, in the grass, in the peacefullest time,
Without that monument of cat,
The cat forgotten in the moon;

And to feel that the light is a rabbit-light,
In which everything is meant for you
And nothing need be explained;

Then there is nothing to think of. It comes of itself;
And east rushes west and west rushes down,
No matter. The grass is full

And full of yourself. The trees around are for you,
The whole of the wideness of night is for you,
A self that touches all edges,

You become a self that fills the four corners of night,
The red cat hides away in the fur-light
And there you are humped high, humped up,

You are humped higher and higher, black as stone—
You sit with your head like a carving in space
And the little green cat is a bug in the grass.

Wallace Stevens

HAWK ROOSTING

I sit in the top of the wood, my eyes closed.
Inaction, no falsifying dream
Between my hooked head and hooked feet:
Or in sleep rehearse perfect kills and eat.

The convenience of the high trees!
The air's buoyancy and the sun's ray
Are of advantage to me;
And the earth's face upward for my inspection.

My feet are locked upon the rough bark.
It took the whole of Creation
To produce my foot, my each feather:
Now I hold Creation in my foot

Or fly up, and revolve it all slowly–
I kill where I please because it is all mine.
There is no sophistry in my body:
My manners are tearing off heads–

The allotment of death.
For the one path of my flight is direct
Through the bones of the living.
No arguments assert my right:

The sun is behind me.
Nothing has changed since I began.
My eye has permitted no change.
I am going to keep things like this.

Ted Hughes

AN ENGLYN ON A YELLOW GREYHOUND

Hound yellow, light of tread—the cunning foe
Of deer bedappled red;
He of the wind gets not ahead,
Nor yet is by the wind outsped.

William Barnes

englyn: a four line stanza in Welsh poetry

THE DOLPHIN'S TOMB

Never again rejoicing in the surges that I sunder
    Shall I toss my neck aloft, as I leap from gulfs of sea;
Nor, circling round a galley, at its fair prow snort with wonder,
    Proud to find it fashioned in the shape of me.
For the dark-blue rollers hurled me high on the land's dry breast
And in this narrow shingle I am laid to rest.

Anyte of Tegea

TRANSLATED FROM THE GREEK BY
F. L. Lucas

shingle: stony beach

THE FISH

In a cool curving world he lies
And ripples with dark ecstasies.
The kind luxurious lapse and steal
Shapes all his universe to feel
And know and be; the clinging stream
Closes his memory, glooms his dream,
Who lips the roots o' the shore, and glides
Superb on unreturning tides.
Those silent waters weave for him
A fluctuant mutable world and dim,
Where wavering masses bulge and gape
Mysterious, and shape to shape
Dies momently through whorl and hollow,
And form and line and solid follow
Solid and line and form to dream
Fantastic down the eternal stream;
An obscure world, a shifting world,
Bulbous, or pulled to thin, or curled,
Or serpentine, or driving arrows,
Or serene slidings, or March narrows.
There slipping wave and shore are one,
And weed and mud. No ray of sun,
But glow to glow fades down the deep
(As dream to unknown dream in sleep);
Shaken translucency illumes
The hyaline of drifting glooms;
The strange soft-handed depth subdues
Drowned colour there, but black to hues,

As death to living, decomposes—
Red darkness of the heart of roses,
Blue brilliant from dead starless skies,
And gold that lies behind the eyes,
The unknown unnameable sightless white
That is the essential flame of night,
Lustreless purple, hooded green,
The myriad hues that lie between
Darkness and darkness! . . .
But there the night is close, and there
Darkness is cold and strange and bare;
And the secret deeps are whisperless;
And rhythm is all deliciousness;
And joy is in the throbbing tide,
Whose intricate fingers beat and glide
In felt bewildering harmonies
Of trembling touch; and music is
The exquisite knocking of the blood.
Space is no more, under the mud;
His bliss is older than the sun.
Silent and straight the waters run.
The lights, the cries, the willows dim,
And the dark tide are one with him.

Rupert Brooke

from *The Fish*

hyaline: smooth sea

THE TORTOISE IN ETERNITY

Within my house of patterned horn
I sleep in such a bed
As men may keep before they're born
And after they are dead.

Sticks and stones may break their bones,
And words may make them bleed;
There is not one of them who owns
An armour to his need.

Tougher than hide or lozenged bark,
Snow-storm and thunder proof,
And quick with sun, and thick with dark,
Is this my darling roof.

Men's troubled dreams of death and birth
Pulse mother-o'-pearl to black;
I bear the rainbow bubble Earth
Square on my scornful back.

Elinor Wylie

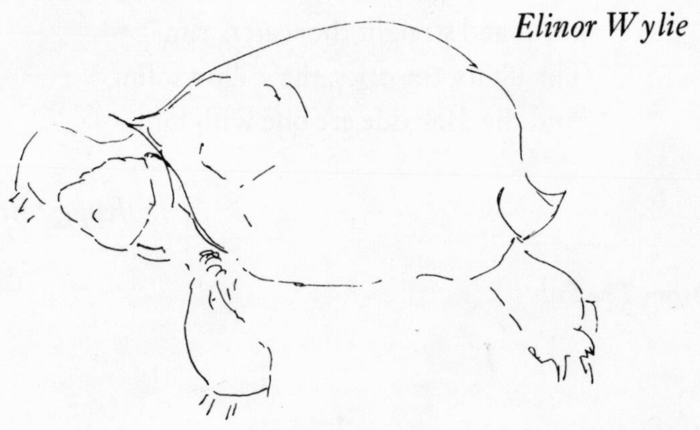

THE WHALE

Now I will fashion   the tale of a fish,
With wise wit singing   in measured strains
The song of the Great Whale.   Often unwittingly
Ocean-mariners   meet with this monster,
Fastitocalon,   fierce and menacing,
The Great Sea-Swimmer   of the ocean-streams.
Like a rough rock   is the Whale's appearance,
Or as if there were swaying   by the shore of the sea
A great mass of sedge   in the midst of the sand dunes;
So it seems to sailors   they see an island,
And they firmly fasten   their high-prowed ships
With anchor-ropes   to the land that is no land,
Hobble their sea-steeds   at ocean's end,
Land bold on the island   and leave their barks
Moored at the water's edge   in the wave's embrace.
There they encamp,   the sea-weary sailors,
Fearing no danger.   They kindle a fire;
High on the island   the hot flames blaze
And joy returns   to travel-worn hearts
Eager for rest.   Then, crafty in evil,
When the Whale feels the sailors   are fully set
And firmly lodged,   enjoying fair weather,
Suddenly with his prey   Ocean's Guest plunges
Down in the salt wave   seeking the depths,
In the hall of death   drowning sailors and ships.

Anonymous

TRANSLATED FROM OLD ENGLISH BY
Charles W. Kennedy

from *Physiologus*

I HEAR THE CRANE

"I hear the crane (if I mistake not) cry:
Who in the clouds forming the forkèd *Y*,
By the brave orders practiz'd under her,
Instructeth souldiers in the art of war.
For when her troops of wandring cranes forsake
Frost-firmèd Strymon, and (in Autumn) take
Truce with the northern dwarfs, to seek adventure
In southern climates for a milder winter;
A front each band a forward captain flies,
Whose pointed bill cuts passage through the skies;
Two skilfull sergeants keep the ranks aright,
And with their voyce hasten their tardy flight;
And when the honey of care-charming sleep
Sweetly begins through all their veines to creep,
One keeps the watch, and ever carefull-most,
Walks many a round about the sleeping hoast,
Still holding in his claw a stony clod,
Whose fall may wake him if he hap to nod;
Another doth as much, a third, a fourth,
Untill, by turns the night be turnèd forth.

Joshua Sylvester

from *Du Bartas His Divine Weeks*

Strymon: river in Bulgaria and Greece

HORSES ON THE CAMARGUE

To A. F. Tschiffely

In the grey wastes of dread,
The haunt of shattered gulls where nothing moves
But in a shroud of silence like the dead,
I heard a sudden harmony of hooves,
And, turning, saw afar
A hundred snowy horses unconfined,
The silver runaways of Neptune's car
Racing, spray-curled, like waves before the wind.
Sons of the Mistral, fleet
As him with whose strong gusts they love to flee,
Who shod the flying thunders on their feet
And plumed them with the snortings of the sea,
Theirs is no earthly breed
Who only haunt the verges of the earth
And only on the sea's salt herbage feed—
Surely the great white breakers gave them birth.
For when for years a slave,
A horse of the Camargue, in alien lands,
Should catch some far-off fragrance of the wave
Carried far inland from his native sands,
Many have told the tale
Of how in fury, foaming at the rein,
He hurls his rider; and with lifted tail,
With coal-red eyes and cataracting mane,
Heading his course for home,
Though sixty foreign leagues before him sweep,
Will never rest until he breathes the foam
And hears the native thunder of the deep.

But when the great gusts rise
And lash their anger on these arid coasts,
When the scared gulls career with mournful cries
And whirl across the waste like driven ghosts:
When hail and fire converge,
The only souls to which they strike no pain
Are the white-crested fillies of the surge
And the white horses of the windy plain.
Then in their strength and pride
The stallions of the wilderness rejoice;
They feel their Master's trident in their side,
And high and shrill they answer to his voice.
With white tails smoking free,
Long streaming manes, and arching necks, they show
Their kinship to their sisters of the sea—
And forward hurl their thunderbolts of snow.
Still out of hardship bred,
Spirits of power and beauty and delight
Have ever on such frugal pastures fed
And loved to course with tempests through the night.

Roy Campbell

Camargue: plain at mouth of the Rhone River in Southern France
mistral: violent, cold, dry wind blowing from the Alps to the Mediterranean

TO A FISH

You strange, astonished-looking, angle-faced,
   Dreary-mouthed, gaping wretches of the sea,
   Gulping salt-water everlastingly,
Cold-blooded, though with red your blood be graced,
And mute, though dwellers in the roaring waste;
   And you, all shapes beside that fishy be,—
   Some round, some flat, some long, all devilry,
Legless, unloving, infamously chaste:—

O scaly, slippery, wet, swift, staring wights,
   What is't ye do? What life lead? eh, dull goggles?
How do ye vary your vile days and nights?
   How pass your Sundays? Are ye still but joggles
In ceaseless wash? Still nought but gapes, and bites,
   And drinks, and stares, diversified with boggles?

Leigh Hunt

boggle: start with fright
goggle: one who squints, rolls eyes around

A FISH ANSWERS

Amazing monster! that, for aught I know,
  With the first sight of thee didst make our race
  For ever stare! O flat and shocking face,
Grimly divided from the breast below!
Thou that on dry land horribly dost go
  With a split body and most ridiculous pace,
  Prong after prong, disgracer of all grace,
Long-useless-finned, haired, upright, unwet, slow!

O breather of unbreathable, sword-sharp air,
  How canst exist? How bear thyself, thou dry
And dreary sloth? What particle canst share
  Of the only blessed life, the watery?
I sometimes see of ye an actual *pair*
  Go by! linked fin by fin! most odiously.

Leigh Hunt

THE DEAD CRAB

A rosy shield upon its back,
That not the hardest storm could crack,
From whose sharp edge projected out
Black pin-point eyes staring about;
Beneath, the well-knit cote-armure
That gave to its weak belly power;
The clustered legs with plated joints
That ended in stiletto points;
The claws like mouths it held outside:
I cannot think this creature died
By storm or fish or sea-fowl harmed
Walking the sea so heavily armed;
Or does it make for death to be
Oneself a living armoury?

Andrew Young

cote-armure: vest worn by knights over their armour

THE EAGLE AND THE MOLE

Avoid the reeking herd,
Shun the polluted flock,
Live like that stoic bird,
The eagle of the rock.

The huddled warmth of crowds
Begets and fosters hate;
He keeps, above the clouds,
His cliff inviolate.

When flocks are folded warm,
And herds to shelter run,
He sails above the storm,
He stares into the sun.

If in the eagle's track
Your sinews cannot leap,
Avoid the lathered pack,
Turn from the steaming sheep.

If you would keep your soul
From spotted sight or sound,
Live like the velvet mole;
Go burrow underground.

And there hold intercourse
With roots of trees and stones,
With rivers at their source,
And disembodied bones.

Elinor Wylie

THE TERMITES

Blind to all reasoned aim, this furtive folk
Breed to destroy, destroy to breed once more,
As they go gnawing tunnels in the floor
That turn to yellow dust as fine as smoke.
Sometimes a hushing slide within the core
Of beams gave warning where some fiber broke,
And someone said, "This house is solid oak:
No fear, it's stood two centuries and more."
And still the midnight work advanced, and still
The sleepers in their forebears' house slept on,
Til the house sank and vanished; roof to sill,
It fell to dust—all but the termites gone;
And these devoured each other or took flight
To scatter more destruction through the night.

Robert Hillyer

JULIUS CAESAR AND THE HONEY-BEE

Poring on Caesar's death with earnest eye,
I heard a fretful buzzing on the pane:
"Poor Bee!" I cried, "I'll help thee by-and-by";
Then dropped mine eyes upon the page again.
Alas, I did not rise; I helped him not:
In the great voice of Roman history
I lost the pleading of the window-bee,
And all his woes and troubles were forgot.
In pity for the mighty chief, who bled
Beside his rival's statue, I delayed
To serve the little insect's present need;
And so he died for lack of human aid.
I could not change the Roman's destiny;
I might have set the honey-maker free.

Charles Tennyson Turner

THE CAMEL

Lord,
do not be displeased.
There *is* something to be said for pride
against thirst, mirages,
and sandstorms;
and I must say
that, to face and rise above
these arid desert dramas,
two humps
are not too many,
nor an arrogant lip.
Some people criticize
my four flat feet,
the bases of my pile of joints,
but what should I do
with high heels
crossing so much country,
such shifting dreams,
while upholding my dignity?
My heart wrung
by the cries of jackals and hyenas,
by the burning silence,
the magnitude of Your cold stars,
I give you thanks, Lord,
for this my realm,
wide as my longings
and the passage of my steps.

Carrying my royalty
in the aristocratic curve of my neck
from oasis to oasis,
one day shall I find again
the caravan of the magi?
And the gates of Your paradise?

Amen

Carmen Bernos de Gasztold

TRANSLATED FROM THE FRENCH BY
Rumer Godden

FOOT, FIN OR FEATHER

For every thing that moves and lives,
Foot, fin, or feather, meat he gives,
He deals the beasts their food
Both in the wilderness and stall,
And hears the raven's urgent call,
And stills her clam'rous brood.

And yet his maker has no need
Of the train'd ox, or prancing steed;
Tho' thunder cloath his chest;
And man that manages the rein,
Is but a creature brief and vain
With such proportion blest.

Christopher Smart

from *Psalm CXLVII*

THE ADVENTURES OF OBERON, KING OF THE FAIRIES, WHILE SEARCHING FOR QUEEN MAB

And tell how Oberon doth fare,
Who grew as mad as any hare
When he had sought each place with care
And found his Queen was missing. . . .

So first encountering with a Wasp,
He in his arms the fly doth clasp
As though his breath he forth would grasp,
Him for Pigwiggen taking:
"Where is my wife, thou rogue?" quoth he;
"Pigwiggen, she is come to thee;
Restore her, or thou diest by me!"
Whereat the poor Wasp quaking

Cries, "Oberon, great Fairy King,
Content thee, I am no such thing:
I am a Wasp, behold my sting!"
At which the Fairy started;
When soon away the Wasp doth go,
Poor wretch, was never frighted so;
He thought his wings were much too slow,
O'erjoyed they so were parted.

He next upon a Glow-worm light,
(You must suppose it now was night),
Which, for her hinder part was bright,
He took to be a devil,

And furiously doth her assail
For carrying fire in her tail;
He thrashed her rough coat with his flail;
    The mad King feared no evil.

"Oh!" quoth the Glow-worm, "hold thy hand,
Thou puissant King of Fairy-land!
Thy mighty strokes who may withstand?
    Hold, or of life despair I!"
Together then herself doth roll,
And tumbling down into a hole
She seemed as black as any coal;
    Which vext away the Fairy.

From thence he ran into a hive:
Amongst the bees he letteth drive,
And down their combs begins to rive,
    All likely to have spoiléd,
Which with their honey daubed his beard:
It would have made a man afeared
    To see how he was moiléd.

A new adventure him betides;
He met an Ant, which he bestrides,
And post thereon away he rides,
    Which with his haste doth stumble;
And came full over on her snout,
Her heels so threw the dirt about,
For she by no means could get out,
    But over him doth tumble.

And being in this piteous case,
And all be-slurred head and face,
On runs he in this wild-goose chase,
    As here and there he rambles;
Half blind, against a molehill hit,
And for a mountain taking it,
For all he was out of his wit
    Yet to the top he scrambles.

And being gotten to the top,
Yet there himself he could not stop,
But down the other side doth chop,
    And to the foot came rumbling;
So that the grubs, therein that bred,
Hearing such turmoil overhead,
Thought surely they had all been dead;
    So fearful was the jumbling.

Michael Drayton

from *Nymphidia, The Court of Fairy*

rive: strike down
moiled: soiled, made sticky

THE ASS IN THE LION'S SKIN

An Ass put on a Lion's skin and went
About the forest with much merriment,
Scaring the foolish beasts by brooks and rocks,
Till at last he tried to scare the Fox.
But Reynard, hearing from beneath the mane
That raucous voice so petulant and vain,
Remarked, 'O Ass, I too would run away,
But that I know your old familiar bray.'

That's just the way with asses, just the way.

Aesop

RENDERED INTO VERSE BY
William Ellery Leonard

AFAR IN THE DESERT

from *Afar in the Desert*

Afar in the desert I love to ride,
With the silent Bush-boy alone by my side,
Away, away from the dwellings of men,
By the wild deer's haunt, by the buffalo's glen;
By valleys remote where the oribi plays,
Where the gnu, the gazelle, and the hartebeest graze,
And the kudu and eland unhunted recline
By the skirts of gray forest o'erhung with wild vine;
Where the elephant browses at peace in his wood,
And the river-horse gambols unscared in the flood,
And the mighty rhinoceros wallows at will
In the fen where the wild ass is drinking his fill.

Afar in the desert I love to ride,
With the silent Bush-boy alone by my side,
O'er the brown karroo, where the bleating cry
Of the springbok's fawn sounds plaintively;
And the timorous quagga's shrill whistling neigh
Is heard by the fountain at twilight gray;
Where the zebra wantonly tosses his mane,
With wild hoof scouring the desolate plain;
And the fleet-footed ostrich over the waste
Speeds like a horseman who travels in haste,
Hieing away to the home of her rest,
Where she and her mate have scooped their nest,
Far hid from the pitiless plunderer's view
In the pathless depths of the parched karroo.

Thomas Pringle

oribi: small species of antelope
quagga: mammal related to the ass and zebra

THE UNICORN'S HOOFS

The unicorn's hoofs!
The duke's sons throng.
Alas for the unicorn!

The unicorn's brow!
The duke's kinsmen throng.
Alas for the unicorn!

The unicorn's horn!
The duke's clansmen throng.
Alas for the unicorn!

Anonymous

TRANSLATED FROM THE CHINESE BY
Arthur Waley

LIMITS

Who knows this or that?
Hark in the wall to the rat:
Since the world was, he has gnawed;
Of his wisdom, of his fraud
What dost thou know?
In the wretched little beast
Is life and heart,
Child and parent,
Not without relation
To fruitful field and sun and moon.
What art thou? His wicked eye
Is cruel to thy cruelty.

Ralph Waldo Emerson

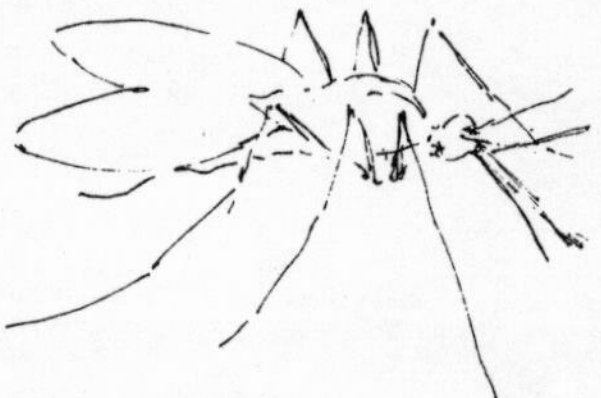

THE MOSQUITO KNOWS–

The mosquito knows full well, small as he is
he's a beast of prey.
But after all
he only takes his bellyful,
he doesn't put my blood in the bank.

D. H. Lawrence

SHE SIGHTS A BIRD

She sights a bird, she chuckles,
She flattens, then she crawls,
She runs without the look of feet,
Her eyes increase to balls,

Her jaws stir, twitching, hungry,
Her teeth can hardly stand.
She leaps–but robin leaps the first!
Ah, pussy of the sand,

The hopes so juicy ripening
You almost bathed your tongue
When bliss dissolved a hundred wings
And fled with every one!

Emily Dickinson

THE ORB WEAVER

Here is the spinner, the orb weaver,
Devised of jet, embossed with sulphur,
Hanging among the fruits of summer,

Hour after hour serenely sullen,
Ripening as September ripens,
Plumping like a grape or melon.

And in its winding-sheet the grasshopper.

The art, the craftsmanship, the cunning,
The patience, the self-control, the waiting,
The sudden dart and the needled poison.

I have no quarrel with the spider
But with the mind or mood that made her
To thrive in nature and in man's nature.

Robert Francis

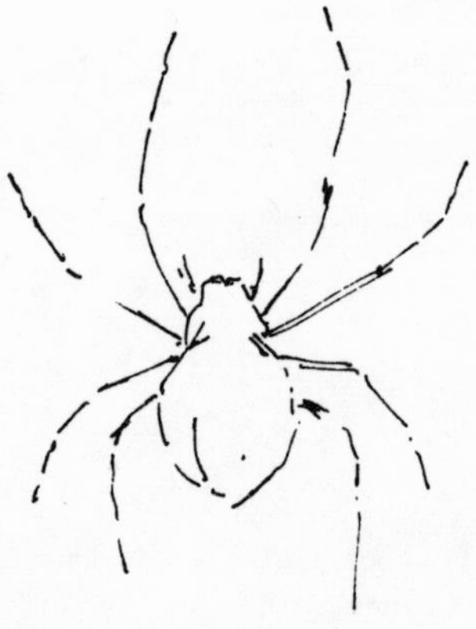

THE PIKE

And nigh this toppling reed, still as the dead
The great pike lies, the murderous patriarch,
Watching the waterpit shelving and dark
Where through the plash his lithe bright vassals thread.

The rose-finned roach and bluish bream
And staring ruffe steal up the stream
Hard by their glutted tyrant, now
Still as a sunken bough.

He on the sandbank lies,
Sunning himself long hours
With stony gorgon eyes:
Westward the hot sun lowers.

Sudden the grey pike changes, and quivering poises for slaughter;
Intense terror wakens round him, the shoals scud awry, but there chances
A chub unsuspecting; the prowling fins quicken, in fury he lances;
And the miller that opens the hatch stands amazed at the whirl in the water.

Edmund Blunden

from *The Pike*

patriarch: ruler
roach, bream, ruffe, chub: kinds of fish

UPON A SPIDER CATCHING A FLY

Thou sorrow, venom Elfe.
Is this thy play,
To spin a web out of thyselfe
To Catch a Fly?
For Why?

I saw a pettish wasp
Fall foule therein.
Whom yet thy Whorle pins did not clasp
Lest he should fling
His sting.

But as affraid, remote
Didst stand hereat
And with thy little fingers stroke
And gently tap
His back.

Thus gently him didst treate
Lest he should pet,
And in a froppish, waspish heate
Should greatly fret
Thy net.

Whereas the silly Fly,
    Caught by its leg
Thou by the throate tookst hastily
    And 'hinde the head
        Bite Dead.

This goes to pot, that not
    Nature doth call.
Strive not above what strength hath got
    Lest in the brawle
        Thou fall.

Edward Taylor

from *Upon a Spider Catching a Fly*

pettish: ill-humoured
froppish: fretful, peevish
whorle: small wheel on a spinning wheel
to go to pot: to be cut in pieces, to be ruined or destroyed

HUNTER'S SONG

"The foils are pitch'd, and the stakes are set,
Ever sing merrily, merrily;
The bows they bend, and the knives they whet,
Hunters live so cheerily.

"It was a stag, a stag of ten,
Bearing its branches sturdily;
He came stately down the glen,
Ever sing hardily, hardily.

"It was there he met with a wounded doe,
She was bleeding deathfully;
She warn'd him of the foils below,
O, so faithfully, faithfully!

"He had an eye, and he could heed,
Ever sing warily, warily;
He had a foot, and he could speed—
Hunters watch so narrowly."

Sir Walter Scott

from *The Lady of The Lake*

foils: net, snare

A RUNNABLE STAG

When the pods went pop on the broom, green broom,
  And apples began to be golden-skinned,
We harboured a stag in the Priory coomb,
  And we feathered his trail up-wind, up-wind,
  We feathered his trail up-wind–
    A stag of warrant, a stag, a stag,
    A runnable stag, a kingly crop,
    Brow, bay and tray and three on top,
    A stag, a runnable stag.

Then the huntsman's horn rang yap, yap, yap,
  And "Forewards" we heard the harbourer shout;
But 'twas only a brocket that broke a gap
  In the beechen underwood, driven out,
  From the underwood antlered out
    By warrant and might of the stag, the stag,
    The runnable stag, whose lordly mind
    Was bent on sleep, though beamed and tined
    He stood, a runnable stag.

So we tufted the covert till afternoon
  With Tinkerman's Pup and Bell-of-the-North;
And hunters were sulky and hounds out of tune
  Before we tufted the right stag forth,
  Before we tufted him forth,
    The stag of warrant, the wily stag,
    The runnable stag with his kingly crop,
    Brow, bay and tray and three on top,
    The royal and runnable stag.

It was Bell-of-the-North and Tinkerman's Pup
  That stuck to the scent till the copse was drawn.
"Tally ho! tally ho!" and the hunt was up,
  The tufters whipped and the pack laid on,
  The resolute pack laid on,
    And the stag of warrant away at last,
    The runnable stag, the same, the same,
    His hoofs on fire, his horns like flame,
    A stag, a runnable stag.

"Let your gelding be: if you check or chide
  He stumbles at once and you're out of the hunt;
For three hundred gentlemen, able to ride,
  On hunters accustomed to bear the brunt,
  Accustomed to bear the brunt,
    Are after the runnable stag, the stag,
    The runnable stag with his kingly crop,
    Brow, bay and tray and three on top,
    The right, the runnable stag."

By perilous paths in coomb and dell,
  The heather, the rocks, and the river-bed,
The pace grew hot, for the scent lay well,
  And a runnable stag goes right ahead,
  The quarry went right ahead—
    Ahead, ahead, and fast and far;
    His antlered crest, his cloven hoof,
    Brow, bay and tray and three aloof,
    The stag, the runnable stag.

For a matter of twenty miles and more,
  By the densest hedge and the highest wall,
Through herds of bullocks he baffled the lore
  Of harbourer, huntsman, hounds and all,
  Of harbourer, hounds and all–
    The stag of warrant, the wily stag,
    For twenty miles, and five and five,
    He ran, and he never was caught alive,
    This stag, this runnable stag.

When he turned at bay in the leafy gloom,
  In the emerald gloom where the brook ran deep,
He heard in the distance the rollers boom,
  And he saw in a vision of peaceful sleep,
  In a wonderful vision of sleep,
    A stag of warrant, a stag, a stag,
    a runnable stag in a jewelled bed,
    Under the sheltering ocean dead,
    A stag, a runnable stag.

So a fateful hope lit up his eye,
  And he opened his nostrils wide again,
And he tossed his branching antlers high
  As he headed the hunt down the Charlock glen,
  As he raced down the echoing glen
    For five miles more, the stag, the stag,
    For twenty miles, and five and five,
    Not to be caught now, dead or alive,
    The stag, the runnable stag.

Three hundred gentlemen, able to ride,
  Three hundred horses as gallant and free,
Beheld him escape on the evening tide,
  Far out till he sank in the Severn Sea,
  Till he sank in the depths of the sea—
    The stag, the buoyant stag, the stag,
    That slept at last in a jewelled bed
    Under the sheltering ocean spread,
    The stag, the runnable stag.

John Davidson

harbour: trace a stag to his lair   coomb: valley
of warrant: of an age to be hunted (5 or 6 years)
brocket: 2 year old male red deer
beam: main stem of an antler
tine: prong of an antler   to tuft: to beat a covert

THOU SHALT SEE THE FIELD-MOUSE PEEP

Thou shalt see the field-mouse peep
Meagre from its celled sleep;
And the snake all winter-thin
Cast on sunny bank its skin;
Freckled nest-eggs thou shalt see
Hatching in the hawthorn-tree,
When the hen-bird's wing doth rest
Quiet on its mossy nest;
Then the hurry and alarm
When the bee-hive casts its swarm;
Acorns ripe down-pattering,
While the autumn breezes sing.

John Keats

from *Fancy*

AUTUMN BIRDS

The wild duck startles like a sudden thought,
And heron slow as if it might be caught;
The flopping crows on weary wing go by,
And greybeard jackdaws, noising as they fly;
The crowds of starnels whizz and hurry by
And darken like a cloud the evening sky;
The larks like thunder rise and suther round,
Then drop and nestle in the stubble ground;
The wild swan hurries high and noises loud,
With white necks peering to the evening cloud.
The weary rooks to distant woods are gone;
With length of tail the magpie winnows on
To neighbouring tree, and leaves the distant crow,
While small birds nestle in the hedge below.

John Clare

starnels: starlings
suther: to make a rushing noise

THE FAWN IN THE SNOW

The brown-dappled fawn
Bereft of the doe
Shivers in blue shadow
Of the glaring snow,

His whole world bright
As a jewel, and hard,
Diamond white,
Turquoise barred.

The trees are black,
Their needles gold,
Their boughs crack
In the keen cold.

The brown-dappled fawn
Bereft of the doe
Trembles and shudders
At the bright snow.

The air whets
The warm throat,
The frost frets
At the smooth coat.

Brown agate eyes
Opened round
Agonize
At the cold ground,

At the cold heaven
Enameled pale,
At the earth shriven
By the snowy gale,

At magic glitter
Burning to blind,
At beauty bitter
As an almond rind.

Fawn, fawn,
Seek for your south,
For kind dawn
With her cool mouth,

For green sod
With gold and blue
Dappled, as God
Has dappled you, . . .

The shivering fawn
Paws at the snow.
South and dawn
Lie below;

Richness and mirth,
Dearth forgiven,
A happy earth,
A warm heaven.

The sleet streams;
The snow flies;
The fawn dreams
With wide brown eyes.

William Rose Benét

FIRST SIGHT

Lambs that learn to walk in snow
When their bleating clouds the air
Meet a vast unwelcome, know
Nothing but a sunless glare.
Newly stumbling to and fro
All they find, outside the fold
Is a wretched width of cold.

As they wait beside the ewe,
Her fleeces wetly caked, there lies
Hidden round them, waiting too,
Earth's immeasurable surprise.
They could not grasp it if they knew,
What so soon will wake and grow
Utterly unlike the snow.

Philip Larkin

MARCH

The insect world, now sunbeams higher climb,
Oft dream of spring, and wake before their time:
Bees stroke their little legs across their wings,
And venture short flights where the snowdrop hings
Its silver bell, and winter aconite
Its buttercup-like flowers that shut at night,
With green leaf furling round its cup of gold,
Like tender maiden muffled from the cold;
They sip and find their honey-dreams are vain,
Then feebly hasten to their hives again.
The butterflies, by eager hopes undone,
Glad as a child come out to greet the sun,
Beneath the shadows of a sunny shower
Are lost, nor see to-morrow's April flower.

John Clare

hings: hangs

SPRING

The soote season, that bud and bloom forth brings,
With green hath clad the hill and eke the vale.
The nightingale with feathers new she sings;
The turtle to her make hath told her tale.
Summer is come, for every spray now springs,
The hart hath hung his old head on the pale;
The buck in brake his winter coat he flings;
The fishes flete with new repairèd scale;
The adder all her slough away she slings;
The swift swallow pursueth the flies smale;
The busy bee her honey now she mings;
Winter is worn that was the flowers' bale.
And thus I see among these pleasant things
Each care decays, and yet my sorrow springs.

Henry Howard, Earl of Surrey

soote: sweet turtle: turtle-dove
pale: stake or slat in a fence
brake: thicket mings: mingles bale: death, harm

STAY THY SOFT MURMURING

Stay thy soft murmuring waters, gentle Rill;
Hush, whispering Winds; ye rustling Leaves, be still;
Rest, silver Butterflies, your quivering wings;
Alight, ye Beetles, from your airy rings;
Ye painted Moths, your gold-eyed plumage furl,
Bow your wide horns, your spiral trunks uncurl;
Glitter ye Glow-worms, on your mossy beds;
Descend, ye Spiders, on your lengthened threads;
Slide here, ye horned Snails, with varnish'd shells;
Ye Bee-nymphs, listen in your waxen cells!

Erasmus Darwin

from *The Loves of the Plants*

THE DYING CRANE

Lo, in a valley peopled thick with trees,
Where the soft day continual evening sees,
Where, in the moist and melancholy shade,
The grass grows rank, but yields a bitter blade,
I found a poor crane sitting all alone,
That from his breast sent many a throbbing groan;
Grov'ling he lay, that sometimes stood upright;
Maimed of his joints in many a doubtful fight:
His ashy coat that bore a gloss so fair,
So often kissed of the enamoured air;
Worn all to rags, and fretted so with rust,
That with his feet he trod it in the dust:
And wanting strength to bear him to the springs,
The spiders wove their webs even in his wings:
And in his train their filmy netting cast.

Michael Drayton

THE NYMPH COMPLAINING FOR THE DEATH OF HER FAWN

With sweetest milk and sugar first
I it at my own fingers nursed;
And as it grew, so every day
It waxed more white and sweet than they.
It had so sweet a breath! And oft
I blushed to see its foot more soft
And white, shall I say than my hand?
Nay, any lady's of the land.
It is a wondrous thing how fleet
'Twas on those little silver feet;
With what a pretty skipping grace
It oft would challenge me the race;
And, when't had left me far away,
'Twould stay, and run again, and stay;
For it was nimbler much than hinds,
And trod as if on the four winds.
I have a garden of my own,
But so with roses overgrown,
And lilies, that you would it guess
To be a little wilderness;
And all the spring-time of the year
It only lovèd to be there.
Among the beds of lilies I
Have sought it oft, where it should lie,
Yet could not, till itself would rise,
Find it, although before mine eyes;
For, in the flaxen lilies' shade,
It like a bank of lilies laid.

Upon the roses it would feed,
Until its lips e'en seem to bleed
And then to me 'twould boldly trip,
And print those roses on my lip.
But all its chief delight was still
On roses thus itself to fill,
And its pure virgin limbs to fold
In whitest sheets of lilies cold:
Had it lived long, it would have been
Lilies without, roses within.

Andrew Marvell

from *The Nymph Complaining for the Death of her Fawn*

AT AMBERLEY WILD BROOKS

Watching the horses stand
And bend their long heads Roman-nosed
With thick cheek veins exposed,
So close to where the brook's bank shelves
They almost meet themselves
In the smooth water sliding by,
I think it strange creatures so great
Can be shut in by wooden gate
And brook no deeper than my hand,
And not like Pegasus shoot wings and fly.

Andrew Young

Pegasus: winged horse in Greek mythology

NIGHTINGALES

Beautiful must be the mountains whence ye come,
And bright in the fruitful valleys the streams,
wherefrom
Ye learn your song:
Where are those starry woods? O might I wander there,
Among the flowers, which in that heavenly air
Bloom the year long!

Nay, barren are those mountains and spent the streams:
Our song is the voice of desire, that haunts our dreams,
A throe of the heart,
Whose pining visions dim, forbidden hopes profound,
No dying cadence nor long sigh can sound,
For all our art.

Alone, aloud in the raptured ear of men
We pour our dark nocturnal secret; and then,
As night is withdrawn
From these sweet-springing meads and bursting boughs
of May,
Dream, while the innumerable choir of day
Welcome the dawn.

Robert Bridges

ANOTHER SONG OF A FOOL

This great purple butterfly,
In the prison of my hands,
Has a learning in his eye
Not a poor fool understands.

Once he lived a schoolmaster
With a stark, denying look;
A string of scholars went in fear
Of his great birch and his great book.

Like the clangour of a bell,
Sweet and harsh, harsh and sweet,
That is how he learnt so well
To take the roses for his meat.

William Butler Yeats

LADY LOST

This morning, there flew up the lane
A timid lady bird to our birdbath
And eyed her image dolefully as death;
This afternoon, knocked on our windowpane
To be let in from the rain.

And when I caught her eye
She looked aside, but at the clapping thunder
And sight of the whole world blazing up like tinder
Looked in on us again most miserably,
Indeed as if she would cry.

So I will go out into the park and say,
"Who has lost a delicate brown-eyed lady
In the West End Section? Or has anybody
Injured some fine woman in some dark way
Last night, or yesterday?

"Let the owner come and claim possession,
No questions will be asked. But stroke her gently
With loving words, and she will evidently
Return to her full soft-haired white-breasted fashion
And her right home and her right passion."

John Crowe Ransom

THE ANIMALS MOURN WITH EVE

Thus she sat weeping,
Thus Eve, our mother,
Where one lay sleeping
Slain by his brother.
Greatest and least
Each piteous beast
To hear her voice
Forgot his joys
And set aside his feast.

The mouse paused in his walk
And dropped his wheaten stalk;
Grave cattle wagged their heads
In rumination;
The eagle gave a cry
From his cloud station;
Larks on thyme beds
Forbore to mount or sing;
Bees drooped upon the wing;
The raven perched on high
Forgot his ration;
The conies in their rock,
A feeble nation,
Quaked sympathetical;
The mocking-bird left off to mock;
Huge camels knelt as if
In deprecation;

The kind hart's tears were falling;
Chattered the wistful stork;
Dove-voices with a dying fall
Cooed desolation,
Answering grief by grief.

Only the serpent in the dust,
Wriggling and crawling,
Grinned an evil grin and thrust
His tongue out with its fork.

Christina Rossetti

from *Eve*

THE ICEBOUND SWANS

Pitiful these crying swans to-night,
caught by the ebb, or is it drought?
Without water coldly flowing at their breasts,
they, three, must die of thirst.

Without water, the firm, thin, and strong,
beating on their breasts in waves;
the great, bubbling sea all gone—
they are held on the smooth, hard, plain.

O King, who brought the tribes to liberty,
who formed heaven, who formed earth,
release, to-night, this little flock, these swans,
chastise the strong until they grow pitiful.

Anonymous

TRANSLATED FROM THE GAELIC BY
Sean O'Faolain

THE LAILY WORM AND THE MACHREL OF THE SEA

"I was but seven year auld
When my mither she did dee,
My father married the ae warst woman
The wardle did ever see.

"For she has made me the laily worm
That lies at the fit o' the tree,
An' my sister Masery she's made
The machrel of the sea.

"An' every Saturday at noon
The machrel comes to me,
An' she takes my laily head,
An' lays it on her knee,
An' kaims it wi' a siller kaim,
An' washes it in the sea.

"Seven knights hae I slain
Sin I lay at the fit of the tree,
An ye war na my ain father,
The eight ane ye should be."

"Sing on your song, ye laily worm,
That ye did sing to me."
"I never sung that song but what
I would sing it to thee.

"I was but seven year auld,
When my mither she did dee;

My father married the ae warst woman
The wardle did ever see.

"She changed me to the laily worm,
That lies at the fit o' the tree,
An' my sister Masery
To the machrel of the sea.

"And every Saturday at noon
The machrel comes to me,
An' she takes my laily head
An' lays it on her knee,
An' kaims it wi' a siller kaim,
An' washes it in the sea.

"Seven knights hae I slain
Sin I lay at the fit o' the tree;
An' ye war na my ain father,
The eighth ane ye should be."

He sent for his lady,
As fast as send could he:
"Whar is my son that ye sent frae me,
And my daughter, Lady Masery?"

"Your son is at our king's court,
Serving for meat an' fee,
An' your daughter's at our queen's court,
The queen's maiden to be."

P

"Ye lee, ye lee, ye ill woman,
  Sae loud as I hear ye lee;
For my son's the laily worm,
  That lies at the fit o' the tree,
And my daughter, Lady Masery,
  Is the machrel of the sea!"

She has tane a siller wan',
  An' gi'en him strokès three,
And he's started up the bravest knight
  That ever your eyes did see.

She has ta'en a small horn,
  An' loud an' shrill blew she,
An' a' the fish came her untill
  But the machrel of the sea:
"Ye shapeit me ance an unseemly shape,
  An' ye's never mare shape me."

He has sent to the wood
  For whins and for hawthorn,
An' he has ta'en that gay lady,
  An' there he did her burn.

Anonymous

laily: loathsome   fit: foot
siller kaim: silver comb   whins: gorze, furze

THE MOCKINGBIRD

Look one way and the sun is going down,
Look the other and the moon is rising.
The sparrow's shadow's longer than the lawn.
The bats squeak: "Night is here"; the birds cheep:
  "Day is gone."
On the willow's highest branch, monopolizing
Day and night, cheeping, squeaking, soaring,
The mockingbird is imitating life.

All day the mockingbird has owned the yard.
As light first woke the world, the sparrows trooped
Onto the seedy lawn: the mockingbird
Chased them off shrieking. Hour by hour, fighting hard
To make the world his own, he swooped
On thrushes, thrashers, jays, and chickadees–
At noon he drove away a big black cat.

Now, in the moonlight, he sits here and sings.
A thrush is singing, then a thrasher, then a jay–
Then, all at once, a cat begins meowing.
A mockingbird can sound like anything.
He imitates the world he drove away
So well that for a minute, in the moonlight,
Which one's the mockingbird? which one's the world?

Randall Jarrell

SONG OF FIXED ACCORD

Rou-cou spoke the dove,
Like the sooth lord of sorrow,
Of sooth love and sorrow,
And a hail-bow, hail-bow,
To this morrow.

She lay upon the roof,
A little wet of wing and woe,
And she rou-ed there,
Softly she piped among the suns
And their ordinary glare,

The sun of five, the sun of six,
Their ordinariness,
And the ordinariness of seven,
Which she accepted,
Like a fixed heaven,

Not subject to change . . .
Day's invisible beginner,
The lord of love and of sooth sorrow,
Lay on the roof
And made much within her.

Wallace Stevens

sooth: true

MIDNIGHT WAS COME

Midnight was come, and every vital thing
With sweet sound sleep their weary limbs did rest.
The beasts were still, the little birds that sing,
Now sweetly slept beside their mother's breast,
The old and all were shrouded in their nest;
The waters calm, the cruel seas did cease,
The woods, and fields, and all things held their peace.

The golden stars were whirl'd amid their race,
And on the earth did laugh with twinkling light,
When each thing nestled in his resting place,
Forgot day's pain with pleasure of the night;
The hare had not the greedy hounds in sight,
The fearful deer of death stood not in doubt,
The partridge dreamt not of falcon's foot.

Thomas Sackville

from *The Complaint of Henrie, Duke of Buckinghame*

VESPER

Now sleep the mountain-summits, sleep the glens,
The peaks, the torrent-beds; all things that creep
On the dark earth lie resting in their dens;
Quiet are the mountain-creatures, quiet the bees,
The monsters hidden in the purple seas;
And birds, the swift of wing,
Sit slumbering.

Alcman of Sparta

TRANSLATED FROM THE GREEK BY
F. L. Lucas

NOTES

THE PETS

St. Colm (usually called Columba or Columkille) is one of the greatest saints of Ireland but he was not always as gentle as he appears in this poem. He was born in the 6th century into the royal family of the O'Neills. Although he early entered the church, he still kept a goodly portion of his family's proud and violent temperament. He had a passion for writing poetry and collecting manuscripts. Once, coveting a psalter that belonged to an abbot, he copied it overnight in the church where it was kept. When the abbot discovered this, he claimed the copy, which Colm refused to give up. The dispute was taken to the king, who ruled, "To every cow her calf", and gave the copy to the abbot. Furious, Colm gathered an army against the king and in a very bloody battle defeated him. The bishops told Colm that as penance he must win as many souls to Christianity as had fallen in the battle. Filled with remorse, Colm sailed for Scotland to become the convertor of the Picts, and the most gentle and humblest of men.

This poem is one of a series about the saint by Robert Farren.

BUFFALO DUSK

When the white men arrived in America vast herds of buffaloes ranged over the country. Some Indian tribes were entirely dependent upon the animal for food and clothing. One herd, described during the Civil War, thickly covered an area twenty-five miles wide and fifty miles long. But with the building of the railways the wholesale slaughter of the great beasts began. In the winter of 1877-8, one hundred thousand buffaloes were killed. In fact the buffalo, like the Indian, just escaped extinction in the United States.

BOOK-MOTH

"Quoth the bookworm, 'I don't care a bit
If the writer has wisdom or wit.
    A volume must be
    Pretty tough to bore me
As completely as I can bore it!' "
                    —Anonymous

DO NOT BELIEVE YOUR SHAKESPEARE'S GRIEF

But in fact Shakespeare, in *Measure for Measure*, has a character say the same thing:

"And the poor beetle that we tread upon,
In corporal sufferance finds a pang as great
As when a giant dies."

Socrates, the Greek philosopher, was sentenced to death by drinking a cup of the poison hemlock. "As black as hangs upon a cross" refers to the crucifixion.

THE RED COCKATOO

The very sophisticated author of this eleven-century-old poem strove for simplicity of language. It is said that he read his poems to an old peasant woman, and changed whatever words she did not understand.

YOLP, YOLP, YOLP, YOLP

This poem, written from the hunter's point of view, was printed in 1603. In another old and anonymous poem poor Wat, the hare, speaks:

'Dogs they run on every side
In furrows that hope me to find;

Hunters take their horse and ride,
And cast the country to the wind.

'Anon as they come me behind,
I look and sit full still and low,
The first man that me doth find
Anon he cries: "So how' so ho!" . . .

'There is no beast in the world, I wean––
Hart, hind, buck, nor doe––
That suffers half so much of teen
As doth the silly Wat––go where he go.'

(*Teen* means misery).

CROW

". . . all the hundreds of his years . . ." The idea that the crow is a long-lived bird is itself an old one. The Greeks believed that a crow lived for nine generations of old men. Actually we know very little about the life-expectancy of wild animals. Some ornithologists believe that birds have longer lives than mammals. The oldest age reliably recorded for a bird is that of an eagle-owl who died at sixty-eight.

A MARTIAL MOUSE

". . . and by old Homer sung." There is a Greek poem called *The Battle of the Frogs and the Mice*. In Butler's time it was believed to have been written by Homer. Actually it is a parody of *The Iliad* (the mice are the Trojans) and was probably written some 300 years later.

THE BUNYIP

The fabled bunyip, half-man, half-fish, and of enormous size, is an invention of the Australian Aborigines. It lives, supposedly, in water-holes, and its head is crowned with a mass of reeds instead of hair. Because of its habit of coming out of its hole at night and eating anyone it can catch, it has a bad reputation.

SHEEP

W. H. Davies did hear this mournful bleating–and more than once. An Englishman, he went to the United States at twenty-one intending to make his fortune. Instead he met a tramp and joined him in travelling round the country. He made several trips across the Atlantic on ships carrying cattle and sheep, caring for the animals. After five years of leading the life of a tramp, he started out for the Klondike to join the Gold Rush. He fell while jumping a freight train in Canada and, minus a leg, came back to England. Here, returning to "the dream of his youth" he began to write poetry. He tried to sell his first poems, printed on single sheets, from door to door. His work became known when he had saved enough money to hire a printer to print a whole book of his poems. Another of Davies' poems is *The Example* page 69.

OLD BLUE

Old Blue was a real longhorn born in Texas in 1870. After proving himself a natural leader on a cattle drive, he was saved from the slaughter house and kept as a lead steer. From Charlie Goodnight's Texas Panhandle ranch, he led herds of two thousand across the plains, through rivers, right into the shipping pens of Dodge City. Blue wore a bell around his neck. At night the clapper was tied up, but in the morning he sought out a cowboy to have it untied, then set off due North with the herd following. Often he made the trip twice a year, returning alone with the cowboys and keeping up with their horses at a pace of thirty miles a day. He never slept with the herd.

OF THE MEAN AND SURE ESTATE

Usually in the story of the town mouse and the country mouse the visitor escapes and is able to give the moral: "If your fine living is thus interrupted with fears and dangers, let me return to my plain food, and my peaceful cottage; for what is elegance without ease; or plenty, with an aching heart." (Robert Dodsley 1764)

ON A SPANIEL NAMED BEAU

Beau was not Cowper's only pet: ". . . he had at one time five rabbits, three hares, two guinea pigs, a magpie, a jay, and a starling; besides two goldfinches, two canary birds, and two dogs. It is amazing how the three hares can find room to gambol and frolic (as they certainly do) in his small parlour. . . . I forgot to enumerate a squirrel, which he had at the same time, and which used to play with one of the hares continually." This description of Cowper's household menagerie was written by his friend Lady Hesketh. She must have been fond of Beau for, evidently, she once wrote Cowper to kiss the spaniel for her. The following is at the end of one of Cowper's letters to her: "Received from my master, on account current with Lady Hesketh, the sum of ——— one kiss on my forehead.

Witness my paw,

Beau X, his mark."

BRAVE ROVER

"Dogs are faithful; they will stick to a bone after everyboddy haz deserted it." Josh Billings, *Animile Statistix*

Beerbohm was primarily a caricaturist and prose writer. The spirited dog he celebrates belonged to friends and its victims are all members of their family.

THE GARDENER AND THE MOLE

Landor was apparently as "mild by nature" as the gardener. He was expelled from his preparatory school for fighting over the correct pronunciation of Latin, and from Oxford for shooting at a student whose politics he disagreed with. He abandoned a home in Wales because of lawsuits with his neighbors and tenants, and later, charged with libel, was forced to leave Florence. The last years of his life he lived alone with his dog.

ERIN (ELEPHANT)

This is a traditional poem of the Yoruba tribe in Nigeria where spoken poetry is still part of daily life. It has been handed down from generation to generation by mouth. Like *The Unicorn's Hoofs* it might well have been sung at a ritual dance.

THE BESTIARY

Pliny, a Roman who lived in the First Century, wrote a book of natural history that was referred to for centuries. As well as reliable information, it contains much that belongs to legend and the realms of the imagination. The compilers of the medieval bestiaries drew heavily from it. About the crocodile, Pliny says that it "produces eggs about the size of those of the goose, and, by a kind of instinctive foresight, always deposits them beyond the limit to which the river Nile rises, when at its greatest height".

The trochilus, a bird related to sandpipers and often called the crocodile bird, does enter the mouth of basking crocodiles. But what it eats is not the remains of the crocodile's meal but the leeches that grow there, which the crocodile is unable to remove itself.

Icheneumon, or Pharoah's Mouse, is an animal something like a weasel. The tale of its stealing down crocodiles' throats probably springs from its bravery in attacking snakes.

Stephen Vincent Benét was married to Elinor Wylie whose poems appear on pages 150 and 158.

A RABBIT AS KING OF THE GHOSTS and HAWK ROOSTING

These two poems are the only ones in the book that attempt to portray an animal's consciousness. The other poets have used animals as a means to express thoughts about life and the nature of man; to draw a religious allegory or to point a moral; to create a certain mood; or they have simply described animals or used them as characters in a tale. Often they have ascribed to birds and beasts the thoughts and feelings of men.

THE DOLPHIN'S TOMB

Pliny says of the dolphin, "He does not dread man, as though a stranger to him, but comes to meet ships, leaps and bounds to and fro, vies with them in swiftness, and passes them even when in full sail."

THE WHALE

There Leviathan,
Hughest of living creatures, in the deep
Stretched like a promontory sleeps or swims,

And seems a moving land; and at his gills
Draws in, and at his breath spouts out a sea.
John Milton, *Paradise Lost*

Pysiologus means naturalist in Greek. It is the name given to an unknown person who wrote a book about animals sometime between the Second and Fifth Centuries A.D. His book was translated into many languages and, with Pliny's *Natural History*, was the foundation of the medieval bestiaries. Our Old English poet, determined to put all knowledge to the use of the church, has turned Pysiologus' description of the whale into a religious allegory. The whale is the devil, and those who put their faith in him will be carried to the depths of hell.

The story of sailors mistaking an animal for an island appears also in *Sindbad the Sailor*, but there, as in the Greek version, the creature described is a gigantic sea turtle. Whales can be almost island-sized. The blue whale is not only the largest of living creatures, but is believed to be the largest creature that ever existed. The largest blue whale on record was 108 feet long and weighed about 160,000 pounds, but a shorter, fatter one, 95 feet long, weighed even more–about 294,000 pounds.

I HEAR THE CRANE

"... take truce with the northern dwarfs ..." Pliny mentions the legendary battles between pygmies and cranes: "... it is these people that Homer has mentioned as being waged war upon by Cranes. It is said that they are in the habit of going down every spring to the sea-shore, in a large body, seated on the backs of rams and goats, and armed with arrows, and there destroy the eggs and the young of those birds ... Their cabins, it is said, are built of mud, mixed with feathers and shells." Pliny states that the pygmies were twenty-seven inches tall. His description of the habits of cranes is as follows: "These birds agree by common consent at what moment they shall set out, . . . select a leader for them to follow, and have sentinels duly posted in the rear, which relieve each other by turns, utter loud cries, and with their voice keep the whole flight in proper array. During the night, also, they place sentinels on guard, each of which holds a little stone in its claw: if the birds should happen to fall asleep, the claw becomes relaxed, and the stone falls to the ground, and so convicts it of neglect. The rest sleep in the meanwhile, with the head beneath the wing, standing first on one leg and then on the other . . ." (*The Natural History of Pliny* translated by John Bostock and H. T. Riley)

THE UNICORN'S HOOFS!

This poem is found in *The Book of Songs*, an ancient collection of Chinese poems written between 800 and 600 B.C. Arthur Waley, the translator, believes that it was a dance-song. He thinks that the dancers, wearing masks, ended their performance by shooting arrows at the masks of a unicorn—first at the hoofs, then at the brow, and finally, at the single horn.

THE PIKE

The pike is one of the most predatory of fish. No fish that shares a pond with a pike is safe. Pikes will even attack small mammals and water birds. Their appetite is such that it is believed that a ten-pound pike eats two pounds of food a day.

UPON A SPIDER CATCHING A FLY

Although Edward Taylor is now considered America's best colonial poet his work was not known until 1937. He never published any of his poetry and this poem was found by chance in the binding of the manuscript copy of his poems. Taylor left England for America in 1668, seeking religious freedom. He spent his long life as a Congregational minister in Westfield, Massachusetts, at that time a frontier town whose very existence was imperilled by the Indians. All of Taylor's poetry is religious, and the spider is not simply a spider. The poem goes on to explain that "Hells spider" weaves his net "to tangle Adams race" and bring it to destruction "by venom things, Damn'd Sins".

A RUNNABLE STAG

"The wild deer wand'ring here and there
Keeps the human soul from care."
William Blake

John Davidson's life was marked by poverty, hardships, and ill health. He drowned himself at the age of fifty-two.

SPRING

Henry Howard, Earl of Surrey, was descended from Edward I and a member of one of England's most powerful families. He was closely connected with the court of Henry VIII. Two of his first cousins, Anne Boleyn and Catherine Howard, were married–for a while–to Henry VIII. Both were executed by the king. Surrey fared no better. When he was about thirty, he was accused of treason and beheaded. He and Thomas Wyatt (see page 98) introduced many Italian verse forms into English, notably the sonnet. Howard was also the first poet to use blank verse in English. Blank verse is unrhymed lines of iambic pentameter, the metre of the plays of Shakespeare and his contemporaries.

ANOTHER SONG OF A FOOL

"Once he lived a schoolmaster . . ." Yeats was interested in the Eastern belief in reincarnation. This belief holds that, after death, souls return to earth in another body, either human or animal.

THE ICEBOUND SWANS

The children of Lir, a Danaan divinity, were changed into swans by their jealous stepmother. They were fated to remain swans until a woman of the South married a man of the North. The first three hundred years of the spell they spent on the calm waters of a lake. People came from all over the island to hear their wonderful music and to speak to them—for they had human speech. But the next six hundred years they had to spend in the waters off the coast, forbidden to touch land. They suffered greatly from storms and cold, their feathers sometimes freezing to the rocks. At the end of nine hundred years they flew to their father's palace but found nothing but a mound of nettles. During their long enchantment the Milesians had invaded Ireland, and the Danaans had retreated to the Land of Youth. A hermit found the swans and taught them the Christian faith, although at first the very sound of his bell was terrible to their ears. When word of the marvellous creatures spread, a princess of the South begged them as a wedding present. Her betrothed, a man of the North, seized them from the hermit and dragged them off by their silver chains. Their feathers fell away and revealed four ancient, withered human beings. After the hermit baptized them, they died. They did not join the Danaans in the Land of Youth but attained the higher destiny of heaven.

This story has its roots in the period when Ireland had been Christianized but the memory of older gods still remained. Its poignancy comes from the confrontation of two religions and cultures, one rising, the other fading away. The Danaans were the old gods of Ireland who retreated underground with the coming of Christianity. The memory of them still lingers in Ireland, but now they are called the sidhe–the fairies.

AUTHOR-TITLE INDEX